Commendations for *The Thorn in the Flesh*

'R. T. offers a radical view of what God's really up to in our lives. His distilled wisdom from a faithful biblical perspective helps us view our problems God's way up. A must for anyone honest enough to inhabit the real world of difficulty, frustration and confusion! R.T. shows God working supernaturally in the midst of our everyday messy lives. A book of great hope and much distilled wisdom!'

Doug Balfour
General Director, Tear Fund

'In these days, when revival is on so many lips, R. T.'s publication will ensure that while our hearts are in heaven our feet remain well and truly on the ground. Very helpful.'

Gerald Coates
Team leader, Pioneer

'Read this case-book of an experienced Pastor, and you will benefit greatly from his practical wisdom and personal insights on transforming *The Thorn in the Flesh*.'

David Coffey
General Secretary, Baptist Union of Great Britain

'I felt less occupied with my problems and more with Jesus after reading R. T.'s book on 'Thorns'. It is practical, pastoral, perceptive and draws heavily on wide personal experience which authenticates his wise and honest counsel.'

Roger Forster
Leader, Icthus Christian Fellowship

'R. T. Kendall has an amazing capacity for communicating life-changing biblical truth with insight, practical application and disarming honesty. Every chapter of this book contains nuggets of wisdom to help us in our walk with Jesus. Another great book from R. T.!'

Mike Pilavachi
Director, Soul Survivor

'*The Thorn in the Flesh* is a truly remarkable and timely book. I really don't know anyone else who could have written it besides R. T. He manages to combine pastoral sensitivity with prophetic insight and at the same time roots all this in a quality of biblical exposition that is unmatched elsewhere. I heartily recommend this book, especially to those who have been struggling long-term with adverse circumstances and are looking for God-given sense in the midst of their suffering.'

Mark Stibbe
Vicar, St Andrew's, Chorleywood

The Thorn in the Flesh

R. T. Kendall

Hodder & Stoughton
LONDON SYDNEY AUCKLAND

Copyright © 1999 R. T. Kendall

First published in Great Britain 1999

The right of R. T. Kendall to be identified as the Author
of the Work has been asserted by him in accordance
with the Copyright, Designs and Patents Act 1988.

10 9 8 7 6 5 4 3 2

British Library Cataloguing in Publication Data
A record for this book is available from the British Library

ISBN 0 340 74546 0

Typeset by Hewer Text Ltd, Edinburgh
Printed and bound in Great Britain by
Clays Ltd, St Ives plc

Hodder and Stoughton Ltd
A Division of Hodder Headline PLC
338 Euston Road
London NW1 3BH

To Rob and Di

Contents

Foreword

Whilst we may seek to live life to the full, enjoying every day that God gives, the break-throughs in our Christian walk seldom come when things are going smoothly. God seems to choose our dark times – the problems, difficulties, pains, temptations and suffering we experience – to draw us closer to him and deeper in our personal pilgrimage.

R.T., writing with insights drawn from many years of ministry, and his own testimony, speaks to those labouring under trials and tribulations of many kinds, helping us to recognise the Hand of God – then to find how he wants us to respond. It is the extraordinary message of *The Thorn in the Flesh* that the very situations which cause us most anguish can, when seen in the light of Christ, become treasured memories and landmarks.

As I read this book, I was able to identify afresh where God has been reaching out to me in my places of weakness and strain. Then I found my humble afflictions were dignified by his immeasurable grace and I was equipped afresh to pray and respond appropriately.

I have known R.T. for many years and, because of our

close friendship, I have been privileged to know something of the thorn in his flesh. His attitude to it has been moving and deeply challenging to me personally: I know of no one better qualified to write on this deeply profound subject.

Rev Lyndon Bowring
Executive Chairman, CARE

Preface

I have been fascinated with the concept of 'thorn in the flesh' for a long time. A few years ago, one Sunday morning before the service, I found myself almost agonising before the Lord – 'Why is this?' I pleaded. I then turned to my regular Bible reading plan (one that was designed by Robert Murray M'Cheyne – the Scottish preacher of the last century) and found myself reading 2 Corinthians 12. Like golden letters leaping out at me, 2 Corinthians 12:7 read:

'To keep me from becoming conceited because of these surpassingly great revelations, there was given me a thorn in my flesh, a messenger of Satan, to torment me.'

I knew this was the explanation to a dilemma I myself had faced for many, many years. As I say in the Introduction, I've decided not to tell what my thorn in the flesh is. But it was of no small comfort to discover that what had plagued me for so long is best understood as that.

I express the hope that the reader may have a similar breakthrough. I hope also that my chapter headings will cover most eventualities, although I'm sure there are many, many more options as to what one's thorn in the flesh could be.

I want to thank Annabel Robson for her help again. This will have been one of the last books she has edited before moving on from Hodder's. My heartfelt thanks also go to Jenny Ross, who typed the original manuscript. My secretary Sheila Penton has had the continued task of finishing the manuscript – for which I am grateful. I have a host of friends who have read the manuscript, and some of them have kindly given Commendations. I want to thank Lyndon Bowring for his Foreword and for the valuable suggestions given to me by his friend Geoff Ridsdale.

I have dedicated this book to Rob and Di Parsons. They have been precious friends for a good number of years, and they also have their thorn – which is mentioned in this book. They may be surprised that I have dedicated this book to them, but they shouldn't be!

R.T. Kendall
Westminster Chapel
London
February 1999

Introduction

In my book *The Anointing: Yesterday, Today, Tomorrow* I endeavoured to show that every person has an anointing. That is good news indeed, but it doesn't end there: God may want to increase our anointing. The sobering news is that he may choose to do this by way of a 'thorn in the flesh'. This will get our attention and is designed to keep us humble. It has the effect not only of protecting our anointing, but of increasing it.

John Newton (1725–1807) is probably best known for his hymn 'Amazing Grace'. It was just one more hymn to him, for he tried to write a new one every week. He would probably be surprised to learn that 'Amazing Grace' is the one that people sing most today. He wrote another hymn, one that is hardly known today, but it fits with this book. I understand why it is not very popular, and I can't say it is my favourite. And yet it describes me perfectly. It reads:

> I asked the Lord that I might grow
> In faith, and love, and every grace,
> Might more of His salvation know,
> And seek more earnestly His face.

1

'Twas He who taught me thus to pray,
And He, I trust, has answered prayer;
But it has been in such a way
As almost drove me to despair.

I hope that in some favoured hour
At once He'd answer my request;
And, by His love's constraining power,
Subdue my sins, and give me rest.

Instead of this, He made me feel
The hidden evils of my heart,
And let the angry powers of hell
Assault my soul in every part.

Yea, more, with His own hand He seemed
Intent to aggravate my woe,
Crossed all the fair designs I schemed,
Blasted my gourds, and laid me low.

'Lord, why is this?' I trembling cried,
'Wilt Thou pursue Thy worm to death?'
' 'Tis in this way', the Lord replied,
'I answer prayer for grace and faith.'

'These inward trials I employ,
From self and pride to set thee free,
And break thy schemes of earthly joy,
That thou mayest seek thy all in Me.'

Of course, it has been impossible for me to write this book
without considering my own 'thorn in the flesh'. I have
one in particular, but to be honest there are others as well.
It was wise of God the Holy Spirit to withhold from us the

identity of Paul's thorn in the flesh, for this enables each of us to enter into the experience. And without trying to elevate myself to Paul's level, I have decided to do the same. Save for this: you should know that it hurts more than you will ever know, is with me day and night, and sometimes, I have felt, is more than I can endure. Over and over, I have cried out to God to be released from it.

In over forty years of ministry I have met some unusual people. I have probably learned as much from conversations with them as I have from reading books and hearing sermons. One of the most stunning comments I ever heard, almost a throwaway remark, came from one of the most famous ministers in the world. He said to me, 'R.T., the more God uses me, the less I am able to enjoy it.'

This is the last thing we want to hear, and maybe it is incomprehensible to some, but I'm sorry to have to tell you that I know exactly what he meant by that. God has many ways of ensuring that while we enjoy his blessing, we do not become conceited. But in my view, his most powerful way of guaranteeing that blessing is the subject of this book – the thorn in the flesh.

I admit that the apostle Paul is a hero for many of us, but I have to face the fact that he too was open to pride and to taking himself too seriously. But God had a plan; Paul was too precious to be allowed to fall into that kind of folly. And so God acted; this is how Paul describes what God decided to do: 'To keep me from becoming conceited because of these surpassingly great revelations, there was given me a thorn in my flesh, a messenger of Satan, to torment me' (2 Cor. 12:7).

Think hard before you pray for a greater anointing. You too may well end up saying: 'The more God uses me, the less I am able to enjoy it.'

To be honest, though, I must add that there is a singular kindness attached to such an affliction. So too with yours; it is God's hint to you that he has not finished with you yet. If you ask me, there is no sweeter thought: the sheer consciousness of God refining me to a greater anointing for his glory. This causes me to hold my thorn close to me, almost to embrace it and say, 'Lord, I would still prefer that you take it away, but not until it has fulfilled all the purposes for which you allowed it.' I dare pray no other way. And as we begin this study together I humbly ask God that by the end of this book, no matter how severe your test, or how bruising your thorn is, my prayer will be yours as well.

1

What is the 'thorn in the flesh'?

> To keep me from becoming conceited because of these surpassingly great revelations, there was given me a thorn in my flesh, a messenger of Satan, to torment me (2 Cor. 12:7).

> And lest I should be exalted above measure through the abundance of the revelations, there was given to me a thorn in the flesh, the messenger of Satan to buffet me, lest I should be exalted above measure (2 Cor. 12:7, AV).

This statement is probably the most candid, transparent and vulnerable admission that any servant of Christ has ever made. Can you believe that the apostle Paul would admit that he could become conceited? How many Christian leaders do you know who admit to a weakness like this? Could you admit, because of your pride, that you actually need a thorn in the flesh? And yet it is the insecure person who will *not* talk like this. Many of us are far too proud to admit that we are full of pride!

Paul says he was given a thorn in the flesh for two reasons. First, because God had been so gracious to him by giving him great revelations. Paul had an extraordinary experience with God, and whenever this happens we are in danger of allowing people to admire us a bit too much. Paul said, 'I know a man in Christ who fourteen years ago was caught up to the third heaven. Whether it was in the body or out of the body I do not know – God knows. And I know that this man – whether in the body or apart from the body I do not know, but God knows – was caught up to Paradise. He heard inexpressible things, things that man is not permitted to tell' (2 Cor 12:2–4).

Paul is speaking about himself here, and later says so. He thus gives a second reason why God sent the thorn in the flesh: to counteract his tendency to take himself too seriously. He openly admits to this. The way the Authorised Version translates it, this thorn was given to him 'lest I should be exalted above measure'. This implies that God gave it to Paul so that others would not think too highly of him. In other words, the New International Version translation shows the possibility of Paul taking himself too seriously, and the Authorised Version shows the possibility of others admiring him too much. In my opinion, it is written with an intentional ambiguity; Paul is saying both. He needed this thorn; others needed it too. In any case, for Paul it is a profoundly humbling experience.

So God sent what Paul calls a 'thorn in the flesh'. The word 'thorn' is from a Greek word *okulops* that means splinter, thorn, or a barb that is like the end of a fishhook. It was driven right into his 'flesh', he says. The word 'flesh' comes from the Greek word *sarx*, a word that is not necessarily referring to the physical flesh, although it could be. It might refer to that because of the possibility of illness, as we will see later, and that is something that must be considered. But almost certainly by 'flesh' he means fallen human nature, what Calvin would call the 'unregenerate' part of the soul. The thorn was probably something in Paul's life that wouldn't go away. God inflicted this. It was painful, it hurt, and it seemed as though it was there to stay. At least for a while – as long as Paul needed it.

Paul said that he had been boasting of things that showed his weakness (2 Cor. 11:30). If one questions whether Paul has been *literally* boasting of his weaknesses, you might say to him, 'Come now, Paul, I don't really think you are boasting of your weaknesses!' Most people boast of their strengths. Most of us like to say things that will impress, either by bragging or by name-dropping, or by saying things that will make others feel a little bit envious.

Boasting was exactly what Paul's enemies, who I will discuss below, did all the time. And it worked for them, they actually endeared themselves to Paul's opposition in Corinth by this boasting. Naïve Christians in Corinth fell for the bragging that Paul's enemies did continually.

Paul retorts, 'If it's boasting you want, I'll boast!' However, he says, 'I am going to boast of my weaknesses.' That is what he has been doing in the preceding section in 2 Corinthians:

Are they Hebrews? So am I. Are they Israelites? So am I. Are they Abraham's descendants? So am

I. Are they servants of Christ? (I am out of my mind to talk like this.) I am more. I have worked much harder, been in prison more frequently, been flogged more severely, and been exposed to death again and again. Five times I received from the Jews the forty lashes minus one. Three times I was beaten with rods, once I was stoned, three times I was shipwrecked, I spent a night and a day in the open sea, I have been constantly on the move. I have been in danger from rivers, in danger from bandits, in danger from my own countrymen, in danger from Gentiles; in danger in the city, in danger in the country, in danger at sea; and in danger from false brothers. I have laboured and toiled and have often gone without sleep; I have known hunger and thirst and have often gone without food; I have been cold and naked. Besides everything else, I face daily the pressure of my concern for all the churches. Who is weak, and I do not feel weak? Who is led into sin, and I do not inwardly burn? (2 Cor. 11:22–9)

It is one thing to have a marvellous experience with God, and Paul could have referred to dozens of such experiences. We know of eight or ten unusual experiences with God that Luke tells us about in the book of Acts, but Paul doesn't refer to one of them. He refers instead to something that happened to him fourteen years before, and the thorn in the flesh probably came immediately after that. In other words, a great experience came to him fourteen years before, and then – right after – the thorn in the flesh.

What, then, is Paul's point? He is saying very candidly, 'Had I been strong, had I been truly a man of humility, had I complete control of my ego, there would have been no need for God to send me a thorn in the flesh because I could have coped with all my revelations and success.' But he says that the opposite is true: 'God sent the thorn because of what I really am.' He is saying, 'If you only knew how weak, how frail, how fragile my ego is, how I am prone to take myself so seriously', but many of us would say, 'Oh, not you, Paul!' 'Yes me! And the proof of it is that God sent me this thorn in the flesh to keep me from becoming conceited.' And it came, almost certainly, soon after that great experience with God to which he refers in 2 Corinthians 12:2–4.

Before we get to the details of the meaning of the thorn in the flesh, I want to make some general observations. If you can take these observations on board, there will be great comfort to follow.

I must say, first of all, that the thorn in the flesh is a manifestation of God's glory. At Westminster Chapel about three hundred of us are involved in a prayer covenant. One petition we pray daily for is 'the manifestation of God's glory in our midst along with an ever-increasing openness in us to the manner in which he chooses to manifest that glory'. I even pray for it daily not only for my church, but for myself too, because each day I want God to unveil his glory to me and I want to be open to the way in which he chooses to do that.

God's glory is the sum total of his attributes (characteristics). If you only had one word to describe God, then it would have to be *glory*. He is a 'God of glory' (Acts 7:2). In Hebrew the word is *kabodh*, which means 'weightiness' or 'heaviness'. It refers to God's stature. In Greek the word is *doxa*; this means 'praise', but comes from a root word that means 'opinion'. God has an opinion that is worthy of praise. When God manifests his glory he is showing himself, and revealing his opinion – or will. The glory of God is the dignity of his will.

St Augustine said that God loves every person as though there were no one else to love. Likewise, he deals with each of us as though there were no one else to deal with. He knows all about us and therefore knows what it takes to get our attention. The way God gets our attention and brings us to a degree of humility is by manifesting his glory.

But are you ready for this: the thorn in the flesh is actually a manifestation of God's glory. If you too pray for God to manifest himself to you, you might say, 'A thorn in the flesh is not exactly what I had in mind!' But there are many ways God shows up, both corporately and individually. Giving us a thorn is not the only way God manifests his glory, I am happy to say, but certainly this was one way in which he communicated with Paul. And to each of us. See your own thorn as God's weighty stature in your life, the dignity of his will for you at this time.

As well as being a manifestation of God's glory, the thorn in the flesh is a severe form of chastening, or disciplining:

> And you have forgotten that word of
> encouragement that addresses you as sons: 'My
> son, do not make light of the Lord's discipline,
> and do not lose heart when he rebukes you,
> because the Lord disciplines those he loves, and
> he punishes everyone he accepts as a son.'
> Endure hardship as discipline; God is treating you
> as sons. For what son is not disciplined by his
> father? (Heb. 12:5–7)

Disciplining, or chastening (as it is in the Authorised Version), comes from a Greek word that means 'enforced learning'. In other words, when nothing else works, God sends a thorn in the flesh to teach us a lesson.

I will never forget my first introduction to the idea of being chastened. It came at an extremely difficult time in my life. My father and grandmother had turned against me, even though they loved me. It was August 1956. Eighteen months before, when I became a student pastor of a church of the Nazarene in Palmer, Tennessee, my grandmother bought a brand-new 1955 Chevrolet for me. I was the first Kendall in the family to become a preacher, and they were so proud of me. But in April 1956 events took place that made me realise that my theological and ecclesiastical direction would go against the wishes of my family. The upshot of this was that my grandmother took the car back. I remember her words, 'Son, give me the keys.' I did, but I then fell across the bed in her room and cried out, 'Why? Lord, you told me you were going to use me.' Nothing was going according to plan. In that moment I felt an impulse to turn to

Hebrews 12:6. So I turned to it in my little pocket-version New Testament, having no idea what I would read. It said: 'For whom the Lord loveth he chasteneth, and scourgeth every son whom he receiveth' (Heb. 12:6, AV).

This verse gave me some comfort, but the pain did not go away. It was my introduction – not to the thorn in the flesh – to the subject of chastening. I knew God himself was behind everything that was happening. I could live with that. Can you? Just to know that the whole thing is of God. So also the thorn in the flesh is a form of chastening, or disciplining – but a much severer kind.

The thorn in the flesh, then, is from God, and it is a way of making us learn. Nothing else will work for us at the time. So God, who knows this, sends the thorn. It is not unlike what C. S. Lewis calls 'severe mercy'.

It may be argued that Paul having a thorn in the flesh does not mean that we will all have one. That could be true. However, I do think *most* Christians have one. Furthermore, Paul said that he himself was 'an example for those who would believe on him and receive eternal life' (1 Tim. 1:16). In this book, I am not talking about the general trials and tribulations that beset every Christian. I refer rather to a crushing blow so definite and lasting that one knows that 'thorn in the flesh' is the best explanation for it.

It is not the same for every person. But if you are a Christian worth your salt, you probably have a thorn in the flesh. What may be yours may not be mine. What may be mine may not be yours. For some it is a handicap, or disability. It could be unhappy employment – or even lack of employment. It may be a job that you are locked into. It could be an enemy. It could be loneliness. It could be coping with unhappy living conditions. It could be a sexual misgiving. It could be an unhappy marriage. It could be chronic illness. It could be a personality problem. It could be to do with money matters. It could be an unwanted calling. The list is endless.

This 'thorn' may be recognisable to you, but unseen by others. God may afflict you with some sort of impediment – by which you may feel he has stripped you of all your self-esteem – but this could be utterly unrecognisable to anybody else. Why? Because this 'thorn' is for you more than for them. Or it may be for them indirectly. It may be so embarrassing and humbling to you that it will make you a different person, such that others will not have an inflated opinion of you. But it is mainly for you – to keep you humble. Certainly it may end up being for others in the sense that they unwittingly do not extol you as they might otherwise have done. This helps to explain the ambiguous use of the Greek text, which is impossible to translate in a single phrase that captures both meanings. This is why Paul's thorn kept him from being conceited; it kept others from exalting him beyond that which was warranted. But Paul's thorn was mainly for him, and yours is mainly for you.

It is conceivable that you could have more than one thorn in the flesh at the same time, but do not make the easy mistake of assuming that any trial or nuisance in your life could be truly called a 'thorn in the flesh'. And yet it may be that there is one trial or difficulty that obtrusively stands out above all others. I could give a dozen negative situations in my own life, but I've got the one that stands out above all others. Nearly every chapter in this book could describe me in varying degrees at one time or another. But for many, what is described below is so acute and painful that it qualifies for the label 'thorn in the flesh'.

We are almost always talking about a situation that you are locked into. It is one that is not likely to go away very soon, if ever. You will ask, 'Do I have to bear this for ever?' Maybe not, but you could. You are probably, though, going to have it for a while. Paul said, 'I prayed three times that it might go away.' It's like a prison sentence. It may be a life sentence, or it may be for a short period of time. Paul's thorn apparently remained. It will stay with us as long as we need it.

Is there a prerequisite for the thorn in the flesh? In other words, what is the condition you must meet to qualify for this thorn in the flesh? As you will know, the word 'prerequisite', as well as meaning 'what is required as a condition', can also mean 'something that prepares you for something to come'. So how do you qualify for getting a thorn in the flesh? What do you have to do to get it?

If you say, 'I don't have a thorn in the flesh', then I don't suggest you pray, 'Oh, please Lord, give me one'! I can tell you right now that it is nothing you should stand in a queue for. It is nothing that you pray to get; you will pray to get rid of it. I don't wish it on anybody.

The first qualification for the thorn in the flesh is the fact that the Lord has been extraordinarily good to you. If he has been unusually good to you – you qualify. Is that you? Peter says that it is you: 'now that you have tasted that the Lord is good' (1 Pet. 2:3). If you can honestly say, 'God hasn't been good to me', then you won't have a thorn in the flesh. So prerequisite number one is that God has been very good to you. It may not be 'visions and revelations from the Lord' (2 Cor. 12:1), but it is none the less an equivalent dose of sovereign grace; so wonderful that it is humbling for you to contemplate. Have you known that the Lord has been good to you in this way? Has he blessed you wonderfully? If he has, then you qualify.

The second prerequisite is that one of your weaknesses happens to be that you tend to take yourself too seriously. If you immediately say, 'That lets me out', then I doubt that this is true. We are talking here about a thing called 'pride'. We are talking about a sensitive ego. We are talking about one who likes a compliment. Paul says, 'I like compliments.' Paul says, 'I far prefer praise to criticism.' So if you're *sure* you don't have a problem where pride is concerned, then there is no problem for you! Congratulations! You will not have a thorn in the flesh. You're exempt, so forget it.

Now I don't want to be unfair, but if you think you don't have a problem with pride, then you show you have no conviction of sin. The more you are convicted of sin, the more you see of God's glory, then the more you will see how proud you are. It's like peeling the layers of an onion. At first you say, 'I'm not that bad', and later you say, 'I'm horrible.' God peels the layers away – that's why you need a thorn in the flesh.

15

The purpose of the thorn in the flesh, Paul says, is to keep us from being conceited because of God's unusual blessing. In Paul's case it was because of 'surpassingly great revelations'. After all, what is the purpose of chastening generally?

> If you are not disciplined (and everyone undergoes discipline), then you are illegitimate children and not true sons. Moreover, we have all had human fathers who disciplined us and we respected them for it. How much more should we submit to the Father of our spirits and live! Our fathers disciplined us for a little while as they thought best; but God disciplines us for our good, that we may share in his holiness. No discipline seems pleasant at the time, but painful. Later on, however, it produces a harvest of righteousness and peace for those who have been trained by it (Heb. 12:8–11).

Chastening is God's ordained means of sanctification, the process by which we are made holy. Therefore, not all chastening or disciplining can be called the 'thorn in the flesh'. Chastening can come and go. There can be a slap on the wrist; God can deal with you immediately and correct you. That is a type of chastening that is quickly over and done with. So not all disciplining is the thorn in the flesh. But the thorn in the flesh is none the less a severe form of chastening, and it is God's ordained means for our sanctification. It is what is needed to get our attention. It will be what will make you more like Jesus. It is the only way, it seems, that God can bend us.

Regarding God's chastening, there is plan A and plan B. Plan A would be that you listen to the Holy Spirit through preaching and teaching, and after hearing preaching you then walk in the light – you say, 'Yes, Lord!' You take it on board, you don't rebel. You don't become obstinate or stubborn and argue back. That's plan A, and the best way to have our problem solved is through the chastening of God's word: reading it yourself or through teaching and preaching. I call this 'internal chastening'.

Plan B is 'external chastening'. Internal chastening is secret, it happens in our hearts. External chastening is when God works from the outside. It may be illness. It may be being found out, like Jonah (Jonah 1:7–9). It may be through a reverse in your finances. It may be the withholding of vindication. God may take someone from you. This is why I think internal chastening, plan A, is best: when we listen to God in the first place. Sooner or later, though, external chastening is what most of us need. But it has great fringe benefits. Paul says that it achieves in us a far greater weight of glory: 'For our light and momentary troubles are achieving for us an eternal glory that far outweighs them all' (2 Cor. 4:17). It is what will ensure you a reward at the judgment seat of Christ.

I can hardly begin to say how deeply it goes with me that we are going to be rewarded at the judgment seat of Christ. Nevertheless, as well as rewards, there will be an evaluation of our lives. This will be a sobering time for all of us. It will not simply be a case of pass or fail; saved or lost; having Christ's imputed righteousness or going to hell. I want you to know that all the saved will stand before Jesus Christ. 'For we must all appear before the judgment seat of Christ, that each one may receive what is due him for the things done while in the body, whether good or bad' (2 Cor. 5:10). It will matter so much to you then. It mattered so much to Paul; he said:

> Do you not know that in a race all the runners run, but only one gets the prize? Run in such a way as to get the prize. Everyone who competes in the games goes into strict training. They do it to get a crown that will not last; but we do it to get a crown that will last for ever. Therefore I do not run like a man running aimlessly; I do not fight like a man beating the air. No, I beat my body and make it my slave so that after I have preached to others, I myself will not be disqualified for the prize (1 Cor. 9:24–7).

Paul knew of the possibility that he could be an effective preacher, see people converted and see people grow, and then he himself be rejected in terms of a reward. He would be saved, yes, but as by fire (1 Cor. 3:15).

Being rewarded at the judgment seat of Christ may seem unimportant now, but will mean everything then. That reward will come, almost certainly, because God sent a thorn in your side. A thorn in the flesh that protected you from yourself! That's why God does it. I therefore go this far: it is arguably the best thing that ever happened to us.

I am convinced I wouldn't have survived without it. It is what has saved me. It has protected me from myself. Sometimes I really do feel I must be the weakest minister in the history of the Church. When members of my church get to heaven and find out how frail their minister was, they will know why God has sent me my particular thorn in the flesh.

Jim Bakker, the TV evangelist who built Heritage City, USA, was charged with intentionally misleading his followers to contribute money. He was sentenced to forty-five years in prison. He was subsequently vindicated, but not until he had spent five years in prison. Those years were horrible, but it was there that God met with him powerfully and intimately. Though falsely accused, Jim Bakker is absolutely convinced that God put him in prison in order to get his attention. This became, for him, his thorn in the flesh; and he says that it's the best thing that has happened to him. This is the key to the thorn in the flesh: we will say, 'This prison sentence is not fun', but later we will be thankful for it.

The specific purpose of the thorn in the flesh, as Professor F. F. Bruce put it, is to puncture your pride. It is a compensatory puncture from God. Now some people get compensation in this life because they have been deprived. For example, if you have been ill, you may get compensation from an insurance policy to make up for it. If a person has been deprived, he hopes for a little bit of compensation to equalise the pain. And that is what the thorn in the flesh is – but the other way around! It is because God has been so good that we need to be compensated negatively! He has been so kind and gracious that it would otherwise go to our heads. Therefore to puncture your pride, God compensates.

Sovereign vessels (those earmarked for special service

of some kind) get this negative compensation because they have been so equipped. The thorn in the flesh is to make up for a deficiency. That is what a compensation is. A typical deficiency is the Christlikeness that is lacking in us. God says, 'I want you to be more like Jesus and I have blessed you.' If we are totally honest, we know God has been good to us. If he didn't send a thorn in the flesh to compensate, who knows what we would be like!

I can think of many deficiencies that require the thorn in the flesh in my case. For example, I don't have enough faith. I don't have enough love. I don't have enough empathy, caring for others. I don't have sufficient conviction of sin. I don't have sufficient humility. These are things that the flesh by itself will never bring about. I need an increase in faith, love, empathy, more conviction of sin, and more humility.

Left to our own devices, we *won't* increase in faith, love, empathy or humility, or have more conviction of sin. By ourselves, we go down, down, down. So Paul says, 'That's why I need it.' And it's why both you and I need it. It's because of the problem we have with pride.

There was only one way by which Paul wasn't likely to take himself too seriously: that his flesh be punctured. His pride is compensated by a most humbling and painful experience.

How, though, does this thorn achieve its aim? How does it actually keep us from being conceited? The answer is that it protects us from ourselves. If you are like me, you sometimes think, 'If God hadn't stopped me, I don't know what I would have said or done.' I have lived long enough to say, when I see in any other person a weakness, a malady, a sin, or wickedness, 'That's me! That's me – except God has kept me.' It is what protects us from ourselves.

Does it make you feel better that even Paul needed it? But that shouldn't surprise us. Paul wasn't Jesus Christ. Sometimes I think that a lot of Christians think that the apostle Paul was only marginally below the level of deity. I can tell you that he was a sinner saved by grace – as great as any, and worse than many. He wasn't joking when he said he was 'less than the least of all God's people' (Eph. 3:8). He wasn't making it up when he said, 'Here is a trustworthy saying that deserves full acceptance: Christ Jesus came into the world to save sinners – of whom I am the worst' (1 Tim. 1:15). And, if you are honest, you will say that it is true of yourself.

How does the thorn work? Through pain. 'No discipline seems pleasant at the time, but painful. Later on, however, it produces a harvest of righteousness and peace for those who have been trained by it' (Heb. 12:11). It is given that we may 'share in his holiness' (Heb. 12:10). It's not pleasant: it's painful. In this book I will be talking about pain. A thorn hurts. It gets and keeps our attention.

Why would God inflict us with pain? Keep in mind that this thorn doesn't kill us, it only hurts. The pain is necessary because God's glory is a no-joke thing. He is determined that no flesh will glory in his presence (1 Cor. 1:29). To a great extent, the thorn will keep us from glorying in his presence. If there were no pain, we would forget; we would lapse into our normal, fleshly routine.

A few years ago I began reading Luke 6:37–8 every day: 'Do not judge, and you will not be judged. Do not condemn, and you will not be condemned. Forgive, and you will be forgiven. Give, and it will be given to you. A good measure, pressed down, shaken together and running over, will be poured into your lap. For with the measure you use, it will be measured to you.'

Why do I read this every day? I started reading it because God was dealing with me severely over my judgmental spirit. Reading this passage from Luke is a life sentence for me, because I do not trust myself to go a whole day without being judgmental if I am not careful, so I just read it every day. In the same way, the thorn in the flesh is God inflicting the pain to keep us in continuous reminder lest we lapse. It keeps us from competing with his glory. It ensures that we will not take any personal credit and it gives him all the glory.

In a word: the thorn hurts. It is a constant trial, it's ever obtrusive. It's always there, it's a reminder. It's a nuisance. Paul even says, '. . . to torment me . . .' You may say, 'God, that's not very nice.' But to quote F. F. Bruce again, it is to give Paul's pride a knock-out blow. It keeps one's feet on the ground. It keeps me from thinking that I have arrived, that I am good enough, that I am worthy. It hurts so that I might be driven to love more. It is obtrusive so that I might develop empathy and won't be judgmental. Are you, like me, one of those who can hardly keep from pointing the finger? God has a way of sending a thorn in the flesh. It's obtrusive, just to make you aware of it all of the time. It's a reminder of your sin. It's a nuisance that produces humility.

This thorn is paradoxical – something that is contradictory but true. What is the contradiction here? Paul says two things. It seems as though he is talking out of both sides of his mouth, saying opposite things. In one breath he says that God gave the thorn, and then in the next breath he says that the devil gave it: 'There was given me a thorn in the flesh.' God did that. Then Paul turns round and says that it is a messenger of Satan to torment him. How on earth can that be? How can God do it, *and* the devil do it?

In fact, there is nothing new about this. Satan always does God's 'dirty work', if I may put it that way. It was Satan who entered Judas Iscariot who betrayed Jesus, which led to the crucifixion of Jesus. So the devil was the architect of the crucifixion of Jesus. At the same time, God says, 'That was my idea.' 'This man was handed over to you by God's set purpose and foreknowledge; and you, with the help of wicked men, put him to death by nailing him to the cross' (Acts 2:23). 'None of the rulers of this age understood it, for if they had, they would not have crucified the Lord of glory' (1 Cor. 2:8). God takes the credit.

God said to Satan, 'Have you considered my servant Job? There is no-one on earth like him; he is blameless and upright, a man who fears God and shuns evil' (Job 1:8). Then the devil attacked Job, but only with God's permission. In 2 Samuel 24:1, the Lord said to David, number the people; but in 1 Chronicles 21:1, which describes the same event, the devil did it.

It is a paradox. God allows Satan to go so far, but no further. This thorn in the flesh probably will not kill you, it just hurts. God does it; the devil does it. But the buck stops with God.

Paul also talks about the permanence of the thorn in the flesh. He said, 'Three times I pleaded with the Lord to take it away from me.' Now there is nothing wrong with praying like that. If I were honest, I've prayed more than three times to get rid of mine – I dare say I've prayed one hundred times. Surely there is nothing wrong in praying for it to go?

Far worse, however, had Paul tried to remove the thorn himself. It's OK to pray and ask God to remove it, but *we* must not try to remove it. Not that you could, because if you are in prison, you are locked up. So just leave it. In all likelihood, that thorn – whether it is an enemy, unhappy living conditions, an unhappy marriage – is likely to stay for a while. It probably won't change soon. It is a painful situation that you appear to be locked into. You pray that it will go away, but it just doesn't.

What was Paul's own thorn in the flesh? Do you *really* want to know? I'm glad we don't know, or we would be less likely to identify with it.

What is *your* thorn in the flesh? Is it a frailty? '. . . for he knows how we are formed, he remembers that we are dust' (Ps. 103:14). It may be a physical problem. It may be an emotional problem. It may be a personal weakness.

It may be a fault: a defect or imperfection – one that feels embarrassing and humbling. You may have prayed about it a thousand times. You may have asked people to lay their hands on you and to pray that this imperfection would disappear. I myself have done this.

It may be a friend. Sometimes a dear friend can be a real thorn in the flesh. Perhaps he or she is difficult. You want to be with them, but afterwards you feel frustrated or all the worse for being in their company. But you need this friend. You know this friend needs you. It is such a delicate situation. It may be a love–hate relationship. You feel you can't be without this person, but the relationship is always edgy, prickly. You feel a rival spirit around this person. You feel that even discussing it would be spontaneous combustion!

It may be an enemy. This person seems to live to make you look bad! But it may be that your enemy – who keeps you on your toes (not to mention on your knees) – is raised up by God to keep you sharp and careful. An enemy can be your downfall, or the best thing that could have come along at the time. Which one of these it is will depend upon your own reaction to God's thorn at the present time.

Could your thorn in the flesh be that you have known failure? It may have been financial failure. A failed marriage. You lost your job. Or you failed when facing temptation and the whole scenario haunts you daily.

Perhaps someone has lied about you. You cannot defend yourself. People believe the lie. You long with all your being to be vindicated. But God withholds vindication. This could be your thorn in the flesh.

In Paul's case, the most we are going to get is a figure of speech. As more than one scholar has observed, thank God we don't know! If we knew, then 99 per cent of us would think that this thorn was for Paul alone. Paul used a figure of speech, a term broad enough to include any of us. Tertullian thought he knew. He said Paul's thorn was a pain in the ear, or in the head. Chrysostom thought Paul's thorn was a particular person, like Hymenaeus or

Alexander the metalworker (2 Tim. 2:17; 4:14). Over the years, I have come across nearly fifty different views! For example, some have said it was epilepsy; others have said it was convulsive attacks. A very popular view is that it was ophthalmia, because of Paul's eye problem (Gal. 4.15) – some are absolutely convinced that the thorn related to his eyes. Others think it was malaria. Some think it was sufferings as a result of persecution. Others think it was attacks of depression after exaltation. Some think it was the Judaisers (to be further explained below). Others think it was the memory of his persecuting the Church before he was saved (in other words, he could never get over this). We could go on and on.

If we knew what it was, then 99 per cent of us would be isolated. But he has given us a little phrase here, 'thorn in the flesh': a metaphor, a figure of speech. This way, we can all get in on it. I agree with Bishop Lightfoot: that we all tend to think Paul's thorn was the same as our own! Whatever Paul's was, 'I've got it!' So if you think it's a fault, you immediately say, 'Paul had a fault; his and mine are the same.' I can only repeat that for the good of the Church, Paul doesn't tell us.

Don't despise your thorn, whatever it is. Don't resent it. It exists by God's sovereign pleasure. It is for our good. It is the best thing that ever happened to us next to our conversion and anointing. It is only a matter of time before we will appreciate it.

2

Loneliness

In May 1984 Billy Graham spoke at Westminster Chapel. His subject was 'Loneliness'. I remember so well what he said. He took his text from a strange verse, Psalm 102, verse 6, in the Authorised Version, where it refers to a pelican in the wilderness, an owl in the desert. Here was a man really in touch with people; he hit a nerve. There are so many people who are lonely.

I remember talking to a lady in the vestry some time ago, and as I listened I thought to myself, 'She hasn't told me why she is here.' She wanted to see me, wanted to talk, and I listened and nodded and thought, 'Is she going to tell me why she is here?' I thought it wasn't going to happen at all when all of a sudden she burst into tears and sobbed, 'I am so lonely!'

It's a very painful condition, a dreaded state. Loneliness is enforced solitude. There's obviously a significant difference between *chosen* solitude and *enforced* solitude. Some of us need the bliss of solitude. Jesus needed to get away from the crowds, and there are some who are by nature loners; they love it that way. My friend Robert Amess calls himself 'the complete loner', but he's not *lonely*.

But there is also self-inflicted loneliness. So often there are those who come into my vestry, whom I know I could help. But they don't want help. Many people – we can all be like this – don't want their problems solved, they want them understood. I remember a lady in my church in Fort Lauderdale who complained to me that people were so unfriendly. I passed this on to the deacons, so they would be aware of this lady. They watched her carefully, then they came to me and said, 'Well, she comes in late and leaves during the last hymn, what are we going to do?' So one of them decided to sit in the back row and, during the last hymn, sure enough, there she went. The deacon went after her and followed her to her car and they talked and talked and talked. It wasn't long before she was integrated into the church. But an effort was needed in this case; loneliness *can* be self-inflicted.

But enforced solitude is another matter. It may be that you are confined to one place or one room. Or, in the case of social isolation, you have got few or no friends. The *Oxford Dictionary* says that loneliness is 'sadness because of lack of friends or companions'. It is when there is no one to share your hurts or joys with. You may spend time with people, and that is good as far as it goes. But you are sad the whole time because you know that, in a few moments, in a very little while, they are going to go back to their homes – some to their wives, some to their husbands. But you go back to your lonely place, and turn on the television.

Billy Graham said that London is one of the loneliest cities in the world. He also pointed out (and I didn't know this) that next to divorced people, university students are the loneliest people in the world. Paul said, 'To keep me from becoming conceited because of these surpassingly great revelations, there was given me a thorn in my flesh, a messenger of Satan, to torment me' (2 Cor. 12:7). Loneliness may be a person's thorn in the flesh. As for Paul's actual thorn in the flesh, as we have seen, there is endless speculation. We do not know what Paul's thorn in the flesh was, but it is possible that it was loneliness. He said in 2 Timothy 4:16, '. . . no-one came to my support, but everyone deserted me.' He said in 1 Corinthians 9:5: 'Don't we have the right to take a believing wife along with us, as do the other apostles and the Lord's brothers and Cephas?' You can read between the lines. Whether Paul was single, married or a widower, he said he had the right to have a wife.

He was no doubt lonely, and all you have to do to confirm this is to look at his description in 2 Corinthians 11:25–30 (see pages 7–8). Whether or not this was Paul's actual thorn in the flesh, we don't know. Consider this, if you look through the chapter headings of this book and wonder 'Do I have a thorn in the flesh?' Then maybe it's this one. Loneliness. This may be your thorn in the flesh, sent from God, ordained by God at least for the moment. The devil will use it to torment you, but remember this: there is a purpose in everything that happens and God himself takes the responsibility for it. I can't think of anything more wonderful than this, just to be reminded, 'Lord, you let this or that happen!' There are few days in my life that I don't pause and say, 'Lord, you let this or that happen for a reason!' I don't know what I would do if I didn't believe that. Imagine those who think that things just 'happen' with no explanation or purpose.

Everything is for a purpose, and if I am describing your own thorn in the flesh – loneliness – then God has allowed it. The devil will exploit it, but the loneliness has a greater purpose. You may be surprised, or maybe not, at just how many people you know who are lonely – if they could but admit it.

Being lonely is not something that we readily admit to. Wealthy people are often lonely because they don't have real friends. People want their friendship for the wrong reasons. Leaders are lonely; the buck stops with them. They feel the burden of difficult decisions that will never please everybody. There are also those who want their friendship *because* they are leaders; they never know whether they are *really* liked or not.

I remember years ago, before we came to Britain, reading in *Time* magazine about the death of Winston Churchill's poodle, Rufus. I never forgot the name Rufus because my Grandpa Kendall, R. J. Kendall, was Rufus Jerome. When Winston Churchill's little poodle died, all commented that he was in deep grief. He actually said, 'I have lost my closest confidant.'

There are people near you right now who are so lonely. If they admit to it they become vulnerable, and they don't want to become vulnerable. Or if they do admit to it, they are afraid this will make you reject them. They don't want to put you on the spot by your having to 'fill in the gap', and so they decide to suffer in silence. Often when I walk across Victoria Street, in that area between the Army and Navy Stores and Boots, I see a man who comes to feed the pigeons. He will get perhaps two or three hundred around him; you can hardly walk past. But you are not going to talk him out of that, despite the nuisance. My feeling is, those are his only friends. That's the reason why some people have pets.

And yet the saddest thing of all is the loneliness of sin and its consequences. Sin results in the greatest loneliness that ever was. You know the expression, 'You ain't seen nothing yet.' You may well feel you are lonely, but sin will ultimately result in the greatest loneliness there ever was. You can blame others and circumstances for so long, but 'be sure that your sin will find you out' (Num. 32:23). As Billy Graham said, 'When you die you will die alone.' When you stand before the judgment seat of Christ, you will stand alone to give an account of the things done in the body (2 Cor. 5:10). You won't have your parents, you won't have a friend who will stand there with you, you will stand alone. It may be our loneliest moment. One of the things that will make hell into hell is loneliness. You will pray and weep, but there will be none to help you, and sadly it will last for ever. I thought I should say this: is there a reader who needs this? Have you come to terms with your sin? There is one way and only one way God will deal with your sin. It will not be by making him promises. It will not be by you saying, 'Well, from now on I am going to be better!' It will be only by your affirming his Son as the only way to heaven, whose death on the cross paid your debt by the shedding of his blood. Then your sins will be washed away. There's no other Name by which we can be saved. It means affirming that Jesus died and paid your debt, and if you haven't yet put your trust in Jesus Christ, do it! Do it now! Be sure now that heaven will be your home because there will be no loneliness in heaven.

There are varieties of loneliness. For example, there is the loneliness of solitude – being alone without companions. You live alone. You eat alone. You watch television alone. You spend Christmas alone. Have you taken a look at Psalm 88? Can you imagine the psalmist hitting rock bottom? He has 'bottomed out', as we say:

> Why, O LORD, do you reject me
>   and hide your face from me?
> From my youth I have been afflicted
>   and close to death;
>   I have suffered your terrors and am in despair.
> Your wrath has swept over me;
>   your terrors have destroyed me.
> All day long they surround me like a flood;
>   they have completely engulfed me.
> You have taken my companions
>   and loved ones from me;
>   the darkness is my closest friend (Ps. 88:14–18).

And yet he lived to write this psalm and wrote it for others as well. It may be bleak for you, it may be that there is nothing out there to look forward to. But look at what the psalmist experienced. Have you ever been like that?

> Standing somewhere in the shadows you will
>   find Jesus;
> He's the only one who cares and understands.

32

Standing somewhere in the shadows you will
   find him;
And you'll know him by the nail prints in his
   hands.

                                          (Anon)

Then there is the loneliness of singleness. I think the
hardest question I get in the vestry is, 'Why does God
allow evil?' – to which I just say, 'I don't know!' The
next hardest question I get in the vestry is: 'R.T., why
can't I find a wife? Why can't I have a husband? Why
can't I find a girlfriend or boyfriend?' My heart goes out
to such people.

   Even before the fall of Adam and Eve in Eden, 'The
LORD God said, "It is not good for the man to be alone. I
will make a helper suitable for him" ' (Gen. 2:18). How
much more so after the Fall? I grant that there are a lot of
people who are single and very happy; they don't want it
any other way. But many would like to be married –
they are so lonely. But there is something worse than
being single, and that is being married – but *unhappily*
(see Chapter 8). Part of the loneliness of singleness is
sexual frustration. Sex is a God-given desire. Sex was not
born in Hollywood, but at the Throne of Grace. There is
a physical need for sexual fulfilment. Loneliness only adds
to this, and my heart goes out to the many who suffer in
this way.

   Jesus is at the right hand of God. When he was on
earth he was tempted at all points, just as we are (Heb.
4:15), but I have to say that he resisted. *He resisted*. But it
is comforting to know that Jesus has never forgotten

33

what it was like then. He therefore sympathises now. The difference between Jesus and some of us is that once we come out of something, we forget what it was like. Jesus has never forgotten what it was like. And yet I feel it is fair to say that, as you resist the opportunity for sexual fulfilment outside of marriage, your reward in heaven will be perhaps as great as any missionary leaving home and going to a foreign field. Do not underestimate what it will mean at the judgment seat of Christ when it will show that you refused to give in! In the words of the famous sermon of the late Dr R. G. Lee: 'pay day, some day'!

There is also the loneliness of separation. This will include separation from a companion. I can't imagine what it would be like to be divorced. It must be awful. If my wife were to leave me, I feel that I would die. So what must it be like – losing a friend, or spouse, or being jilted? Or take the case of someone moving away from you. Or your having to leave home, and there is no one around. It wasn't always that way, but today it's so lonely.

There is separation by death, and I refer to that in two ways. First, having to say goodbye to those who are dying. But secondly, there is the loneliness of your own death. I never will forget when Billy Graham described people dying in their hospital rooms; your friends, your loved ones, may gather around your bedside and may hold your hand, 'But you will die alone.'

There's the loneliness of suffering – in sickness, when you are ill and alone, with no one to take care of you. When you are in pain, being alone, no one to share it with. When you are in a deep valley or trial, no one to talk to, what must it be like? Perhaps you have a particular type of suffering or illness, weakness or trial that no one but you has had. You look high and low for some other person who will know exactly what you are going through. You feel so lonely.

That is where Jesus comes in. There is not a single temptation that you can have that he doesn't understand. He sympathises, he never moralises. You may go to another person and they may say, 'Oh, are you bothered by that?' And you just feel awful that you even went to them in the first place. You look for one other person, and sometimes you won't find that other person, or they just don't understand. But Jesus does. Is this your thorn in the flesh?

There is also the loneliness of service. It is when you are serving the Lord in ministry and it can be the loneliest thing you have ever done. Jesus in ministry went up to a mountain to pray and he was there alone. There is loneliness when you have to make decisions or a judgment that isn't going to be appreciated. And so you can be in ministry, doing the Lord's work, but nobody appreciates what you are doing. No one is going to do it but you, and they take you for granted.

Perhaps you have taken a courageous stand, but no one understands. Listen to Paul: 'At my first defence, no one came to my support, but everyone deserted me. May it not be held against them' (2 Tim. 4:16). There are those missionaries who have left family and friends. They have gone to an alien country, away from familiar surroundings. The loneliness of service. There is the loneliness of doing things in your own church. Nobody knows you do it, but God knows.

There's the loneliness of the stigma. What's the stigma? As I put it in *The Anointing: Yesterday, Today, Tomorrow*, it is part of the anointing. It is the offence of the cross. When you are utterly misunderstood and it hurts. When your best friends don't believe what you are saying or they misunderstand your motives. You align yourself with someone nobody approves of. Or they don't like your message. The essence of the stigma is probably loneliness. You are required to go 'outside the camp, bearing the disgrace' (Heb. 13:13). Are you suffering a stigma because of what you believe? Have you lost your good reputation? Could this be your thorn in the flesh?

There is the loneliness of success. When you are successful, you will find that some people will desert you. They liked you when you weren't successful; they thought you were nice. You start succeeding, you get high marks, you obtain a good job, you have a higher income (it's envy of course, that's all it is); they can't cope with that. But *you* wouldn't be any different if it was reversed (you've got to understand that), but you need to know that success means loneliness. Paul said that we should weep with those who weep and rejoice with those who rejoice (Rom. 12:15). But it is far easier to find somebody to weep with you than to rejoice with you!

On the other hand, if you are successful, whereas some will desert you, others will cling to you. But what are their motives? It is not necessarily you they are interested in. Take somebody like Paul Cain when he's in an area where there are Christians. He can't walk across a hotel lobby, can't walk five feet, without somebody coming up to him. They aren't interested in him. They want 'a word from the Lord' from him. In fact, a friend of mine said, 'I just want to meet him, could you arrange for me to meet Paul Cain?' I said, 'Well, it's not easy, but I can see what I can do.' I said, 'He's a lonely man and all people ever want is "a word, a word!" ' But my friend insisted, 'I just want to meet him!' So I arranged it, and the first thing my friend said was, 'Do you have a word for me?' Paul is a lonely man.

When you are successful or well known, you will find you can be very lonely. This was part of the apostle Paul's problem. You see, he was a successful man. He founded churches all over the ancient world; people thought he would not succeed, but he did. For when there is an anointing upon you, you will succeed in some sense. There may be those who are envious of you, and believe that eventually you are going to fall. King Saul was so jealous of David, he would have done anything to get rid of him. King Saul had a great plan. He said, 'I tell you what, how would you like to marry my daughter? But I think you should do something to earn it.' David said, 'Oh, I am not worthy to be the King's son-in-law.' 'Oh, well,' said King Saul, 'I tell you what I want you to do. All I would ask you to do is to bring back 100 foreskins of the Philistines, that's all!' The only reason King Saul suggested this was that he thought David would be killed in doing it; that was King Saul's sole motive. But David came back with 200 foreskins. When there is an anointing upon you, you will succeed at a certain level, but don't expect your enemies to clap their hands. They will hate you all the more.

Consider the loneliness of Jesus. The loneliest person that ever was, was Jesus. It is said that the President of the United States is the loneliest person in the world. They say that Her Majesty the Queen is the loneliest person in the world. But the loneliest person that ever was, was Jesus. Think about that time, at the Last Supper, when all of a sudden the disciples were arguing among themselves, who is to be the greatest? You can almost sense Jesus looking up to the Father, as if to say, 'Hasn't anybody listened to me here?' After three years of spoon-feeding them, teaching them, here they are, arguing among themselves, who's going to be the greatest? They haven't really heard Jesus. Then in the Garden of Gethsemane, he took his closest friends, Peter, James and John, and said, 'Would you wait with me one hour?' But they fell asleep. He pleaded with them to stay with him for just one hour! He came back, and there they were asleep; one of the most moving ways of translating it is in the Authorised Version: Jesus just looked at them and said, 'Sleep on now . . . the hour is come' (Mark 14:41). He just wanted some close empathetic companionship there at the end. He knew he would die alone. On the cross, he cried out, 'My God, my God, why have you forsaken me?' (Matt. 27:46). The loneliest person that ever was, was our Lord.

But there is a value in loneliness. Loneliness isn't for nothing. If you are in a situation of enforced solitude, there is a reason. God does not send the thorn in the flesh for nothing. Moreover, it is not punishment. Don't say, 'Oh, I am getting my dues!' Wrong!

> . . . he does not treat us as our sins deserve
>   or repay us according to our iniquities.
> For as high as the heavens are above the earth,
>   so great is his love for those who fear him;
> as far as the east is from the west,
>   so far has he removed our transgressions from
>   us (Ps. 103:10–12).

God got even at the cross. The thorn in the flesh is not punishment. It is preparation. God knows our frame, he remembers that we are dust.

We all need preparation in some way. Part of my own preparation has been learning to cope with loneliness. When I first became minister of Westminster Chapel in 1977, I am sure that I was arrogant and conceited – probably more so than I am now. I had finished my college degree, I had gone to seminary, I had a degree from Oxford, and then I was called to be here and thought, 'Now, I am ready!' I think God looked down from heaven and said, 'Really?' I now believe that all that has happened to me so far is just preparation. I take comfort from Spurgeon's comment: that if he knew he had twenty-five years left to live he would spend twenty of them in preparation. My point is, there is value in the thorn in the flesh.

There is loneliness in leadership. President Harry Truman was famous for the plaque on his desk in the White House: 'The buck stops here.' But you don't have to be President to be lonely. Every church leader knows the pain of having to make unpopular decisions, the pain of not getting very close to those you minister to, the pain of treating everybody the same. There are basically two types of people: energisers and drainers. A leader needs to be with energisers – but where can he find them? Most people come to a leader needing advice or wanting somebody to listen. A leader needs to relax with people with whom he can 'be himself', but such people are rare. A church leader is often on a pedestal in people's minds, and he feels he must always set an example. It's like living in a goldfish bowl; it is draining. A true friend is someone who knows all about you and *still* loves you!

My own loneliness emerges at this point. So many good people sincerely want to be a close friend to me. But they do not honestly grasp the point that, were they to get to know me very well, they would not like me or admire me as much. If you told them that, they would invariably say, 'But I am one you can really be yourself with!' But I know better! Some get offended when they can't be your closest friend, and they will not understand until we get to heaven that keeping them at a distance is for their own good. You cannot convince them now, though.

I remember one church member who said, 'You need to spend more time away from people.' I agreed. He had the perfect solution: he himself would spend a whole day with me walking in the forest and just kicking leaves. He couldn't imagine why I turned him down! He would have been devastated to discover that he was the exact type of person I needed to get away from! His solution only added to my loneliness. Moreover, had I begun doing that sort of thing with him, others could be resentful that I chose him to be close to and not them. Still others only want to be with you so they can tell others they were with you. Wherever can one find a friend who won't be controlling, like you the way you are, and never ever tell a soul that they are your friend?

On top of this, there is the loneliness of a church leader's wife. She faces the exact same thing. My wife Louise is probably the most popular member of my church; she is greatly loved and admired. But some have been deeply hurt when they can't have more of her time than she is able to give. They feel rejected and bewildered that she has to keep even those that she loves at a certain distance.

Some may say: but don't you have each other? Yes. And I can't imagine life without the times of sharing the very things I have described above. But at times we are both in the awkward position of protecting each other. Louise hears things that she knows won't bless me, so she holds them inside. I face problems that, were she to know about them, would only upset her.

The loneliness of leadership; it is part of the job. President Truman also used to say, 'If you can't stand the heat, get out of the kitchen.' The heat can be criticism, yes. But the pressure of loneliness is also part of the package.

But there *are* advantages to loneliness. For example, you have time to pray; you may never have such time again. Some have time to pray and lament their enforced solitude, and unfortunately hate it. But one day you may say, I wish I had that time now. One reason for enforced solitude is that God wants you all to himself. He loves your company, and you could be lamenting the very thing that he has designed in order to have your company.

Jim Bakker, who, as we saw earlier, spent five years in prison, once spent a week fishing with me. He came out of prison with a guilelessness; he is broken and changed – there's no doubt about it. But I warned him because he said, 'I am getting more offers than I have ever had in my life, more invitations.' He doesn't know what to do. I said, 'Jim, remember in prison you had all the time to pray, take the time now, because you can lose that intimacy you had with God.' Some, in order to pray, are having to make the time. For others, it's enforced; it is resented. You may one day wish that you had used the time to pray. This is your moment to develop two things: (1) to become an intercessor, where you can start praying for people, and (2) to get to know God with an intimacy beyond anything that you dreamed possible.

Another value of loneliness is to make you sympathetic towards others. That is one of the main purposes of any trial. As Paul put it, 'And our hope for you is firm, because we know that just as you share in our sufferings, so also you share in our comfort' (2 Cor. 1:7). It produces in us patient endurance of the same sufferings. You will be able to sympathise, you will be able to identify with another person. Pray you will never forget what it was like, should this thorn be withdrawn from your flesh.

The value of loneliness is also to remind you that your real home is heaven. Abraham, I believe, was a very lonely man. We are told that he spent a lifetime living in tents, but the writer of Hebrews said, 'For he was looking forward to the city with foundations, whose architect and builder is God' (Heb. 11:10). Abraham, the great man of faith, was a lonely man, but he was on his way to a better place. There will be no loneliness in heaven. So don't look at your heavenly Father and shake your fist, but rather say, 'Lord, you know me. You know what I need and I accept that you know what I need.' Jim Bakker was unfairly put in prison. He has since been vindicated, but do you know what Jim Bakker now says? 'I deserved to go to prison for other things, not for the things that they got me on.' He said, 'God put me there, God did it, God meant it for good!' And if you can look at loneliness like that, though it's not fun, you can recognise that the Lord knows what you are like, and what you need.

Is there a victory in loneliness? I don't say victory over it, but victory in it. Yes! You become aware of the presence of Jesus. I repeat, he wants you to himself. He loves your company, but are you giving it to him? He wants to be real to us. But he wants us to want it so much that we will take advantage of the enforced solitude and just be with him. I do not say that it totally takes the place of friends, but his presence compensates. You get to talk to him as a friend. Abraham was God's friend (Jas. 2:23). Moses talked to the Lord face to face as a man talked to his friend (Exod. 34:11). Your victory is that you feel his presence, you become more like him. After all, Jesus walked alone. He forgave everybody, there was not a trace of bitterness in him, he never gave in to self-pity.

A real value of loneliness, especially if you are single, is

43

that you may have more time. You have time to take on more responsibilities, or duties, whether at your church or visiting elderly or sick people. This was Paul's point in 1 Corinthians 7:32–5:

> I would like you to be free from concern. An unmarried man is concerned about the Lord's affairs – how he can please the Lord. But a married man is concerned about the affairs of this world – how he can please his wife – and his interests are divided. An unmarried woman or virgin is concerned about the Lord's affairs: Her aim is to be devoted to the Lord in both body and spirit. But a married woman is concerned about the affairs of this world – how she can please her husband. I am saying this for your own good, not to restrict you, but that you may live in a right way in undivided devotion to the Lord.

You also learn to worship and praise. It is easy to worship when all is going well. Do you want to know something that pleases God? Do you know what he likes? It's when you worship him and you don't feel like it. You praise him and you don't feel like it – you just do it! Oh, he likes that, it honours him.

There was a purpose in Paul's thorn, and if your thorn is loneliness, know that it was lovingly and deliberately designed just for you. If Paul's thorn in the flesh was the best thing that happened to him – and it was – so too with you and me.

3

Unhappy employment

Do you know what it is like to be locked into a job you don't like? All of us have to work to stay alive. Sadly, some people have a thorn in the flesh that is even worse than unhappy employment – they don't have a job at all. Some people suffer the indignity of not being able to find work. Some are suddenly made redundant and suffer the pain of both continuing financial pressure and the humiliation of being on the dole. And yet God ordained that we must work in order to live: 'By the sweat of your brow you will eat your food until you return to the ground, since from it you were taken; for dust you are and to dust you will return' (Gen. 3:19).

Some like what they do when it comes to their job; others do not. I doubt I would be wrong in saying that the majority do not. My experience is that most people aren't happy where they have to work, with what they have to do, who they have to work with. Therefore most people, in a perfect world, would choose a different job. But we don't live in a perfect world. As President John F. Kennedy used to say, 'Life is not fair.'

Have you ever seen your own job, where you have to

45

work, and what you have to do to make ends meet, as a thorn in the flesh? As I've already said, we won't know until we get to heaven what Paul's thorn was. He says, 'There was given me a thorn in my flesh, a messenger of Satan to torment me.' He uses a term that invites all of us to apply it to ourselves. It is when we are locked into something unpleasant – it never seems to end. Like Paul, we pray for it to be removed. All sovereign vessels (those earmarked by God for special work) have at least one thorn in the flesh. For some it may be temporary, for others it never goes away. If you are a Christian, God has put his hand on you. But for the moment, let us say, you've got a job you don't like and you've got no choice. Consider it to be your thorn in the flesh.

The purpose of this chapter is to make that thorn just a little bit less painful.

The thorn in the flesh has a twofold purpose. There is the divine purpose, but there is also the demonic purpose. The two are actually parallel. Don't ask me to explain it, but God permits it, and yet the devil capitalises on it. The devil is there to torment. The thorn in the flesh is 'a messenger of Satan'. What is the difference between the two? The divine purpose is to keep us from becoming conceited; we all need that. If God doesn't put the brakes on, our big egos would get out of hand; we would take ourselves too seriously. Paul said, 'I needed it.' You need it, I need it. The divine purpose, then, is to keep us from becoming conceited, but the demonic purpose is to torment you and to make you miserable and to make life hard. That's the devil's nature.

In this chapter I want to look at this in the light of the

life of Joseph. The story begins in Genesis 39. Joseph was a sovereign vessel, earmarked for something that was far beyond what he was doing at the time. He was a conceited young man who nevertheless had a genuine gift, an anointing. His gift was quite extraordinary. It had to do with the prophetic, with dreams. God visited him in an intimate way and he had a wonderful gift. There was nothing wrong with his gift, but there was a lot wrong with Joseph. He bragged to his brothers. He strutted around in that coat of many colours, which showed how insensitive he was. His brothers were already jealous of him, for they knew that their father, Jacob, preferred Joseph to the rest of them. But then Joseph would talk about his dreams and I think God just looked down from heaven and said, 'Oh Joseph, you need a little help.' Joseph was consequently earmarked for an unhappy period in his life. He was sold by his brothers to the Ishmaelites and he ended up in Egypt.

Joseph was then held captive by unwanted employment: 'Now Joseph had been taken down to Egypt. Potiphar, an Egyptian who was one of Pharaoh's officials, the captain of the guard, bought him from the Ishmaelites who had taken him there' (Gen. 39:1).

So here was Joseph in a foreign country, in a place where he didn't even want to live in the first place. Here is someone who was stuck, in two ways. First, in a country he never wanted to live in, and secondly, with a job he never wanted to have. There were new surroundings, strange to him. Everything was alien, foreign, odd; it wasn't home and he knew nobody.

Do you have to work somewhere you never wanted

to be? Maybe you have to live where you never wanted to live. Likewise, Joseph had no control; he had been bought. The Ishmaelites paid money to the brothers for Joseph and the Ishmaelites probably made a profit. Potiphar bought him. But poor Joseph, stuck.

The job that Joseph had to do was out of his hands. He was now owned by someone he didn't even know. It is the opposite of the so-called 'rags to riches' syndrome. Are you one of those who enjoys reading stories about those who go from rags to riches? Maybe you enjoy even more a story about someone who goes from riches to rags! Joseph was born with a 'silver spoon in his mouth', and then all of a sudden he wakes up and has to do something he wasn't equipped for, trained for, ready for. He doesn't know how to do it! The humiliation of it!

I remember the days when I was living in south Florida selling vacuum cleaners. I never will forget the time I had just sold a vacuum cleaner to a wealthy person. He said, 'Let me bring in my maid so you can show her how to use this vacuum cleaner you've just sold us.' This maid was a Cuban and, as I began to talk to her, she said, 'I was the owner of a home twice this size, but I fled Fidel Castro just to live outside Cuba and now I work as a maid in this home.' Can you imagine what that must be like? That was something that Joseph was experiencing. On top of that, he was 'over-qualified' for this kind of work. He was not prepared to do menial tasks. His gift – a quite extraordinary one – had to do with prophetic dreams.

What is Joseph going to do? Is he going to say to Potiphar, 'Well, I'm over-qualified for this job. If you have a dream, come and see me, but I am not going to get my hands dirty!' As I said, there was nothing wrong with Joseph's gift, but there was too much wrong with him – when suddenly he was thrust into a captivity of unwanted employment. It was to keep him from being conceited! Because that's what he was. And that is what we all are if we are not checked.

Are you over-qualified for what you do? Do you have to scrub floors when you ought to be in charge of an office? Do you have to type letters when you ought to be speaking to large audiences? It was humbling for Joseph to be a slave to Potiphar in Egypt, when he had been given the rights of the first-born a few months before. That is what Jacob had done to Joseph. Captivity. Stuck. Is that you? You're stuck with your job? You are over-qualified for what you're having to do?

There is a cause for undesirable employment. Sin came into the world; it took place in the Garden of Eden. Before the Fall, I don't think work was really hard – it was probably fun. I don't think Adam found it hard, difficult or humbling. He wasn't toiling when he was naming the animals. That was fun. Before sin came into the world, all activity was fun. When we get to heaven it will be like it was before the Fall. We will be busy; we won't get tired. There will be no sleeping in heaven; there will be no night there. It won't be boring; it won't be hard. But when sin came into the world, everything changed:

> To Adam he said, 'Because you listened to your wife and ate from the tree about which I

commanded you, "You must not eat of it,"
cursed is the ground because of you; through
painful toil you will eat of it all the days of your
life. It will produce thorns and thistles for you,
and you will eat the plants of the field. By the
sweat of your brow you will eat your food until
you return to the ground, since from it you were
taken; for dust you are and to dust you will
return' (Gen. 3:17–19).

This is why work isn't a piece of cake. Work was never
intended to be a life of ease. That is the cause of work – it
is part of man's punishment for sin in the Garden of
Eden.

But there is a second cause of work: we need humbling. Have you had the equivalent of a coat of many
colours that made everybody jealous? And God had to
take it from you?

I referred earlier to my grandmother – so proud that I
was the first Kendall in the family to become a preacher,
and how she bought me a brand-new 1955 Chevrolet. I
was one of the only people at Trevecca Nazarene College
to have a car. I can imagine, looking back, and it horrifies
me, that I must have been a pain to other students. After
she took it away from me, the very next month (I'll never
forget it as long as I live), a man by the name of Marvin
Creamans gave me a job delivering dry-cleaning. He
handed me the keys to his truck. I got in and sat down
and put the keys into the ignition and I thought, Wow! I
immediately remembered a vision I'd had three weeks
earlier as I drove in my grandmother's car: driving through

Kentucky I looked at the dashboard and it was like an older Chevrolet. I knew I was having a vision, but it was so real. I recognised the dashboard because my friend Ralph Lee had a similar car. I knew the dashboard well, and I thought, what have I done? Then I pulled myself together and drove on home. That was the first hint that I might forfeit my new car. I had a feeling what it meant, but I had completely forgotten it until, having just been given a job delivering dry-cleaning, I sat in the car, put the key in the ignition, and there was the same dashboard I had seen in the vision. It made me see how God was in control; also, that I was equally in his will.

I now had to work to eat. No longer was I a student pastor. No longer were people saying, 'Oh that was a good sermon!' I was getting no ego strokes! Three months later I learned to sell baby equipment. I was now utterly out of the ministry. That is what I was doing when I first met my wife Louise. After we married I sold life insurance, and then, only because I made more money at it, I became a door-to-door vacuum cleaner salesman. You cannot imagine the humiliation of it! I remember how I would go to church and hope I wouldn't see anybody I knew. If I did, the pain was always worse than I had imagined. I was, at one time, the so-called blue-eyed boy in my former denomination. It was now a horrible feeling. There was also the pain of knowing what my dad was going through. People would come up to him and say; 'Hello, Mr Kendall. By the way, how's R.T. these days?' 'Oh, well, he's selling vacuum cleaners.' 'Right. Well, God bless you, Mr Kendall, I know these are not easy days.'

Unhappy employment was a former thorn in my flesh, and it goes to show that a thorn may be temporary. So I understand what someone might be going through in relation to this problem, except that in my case it turned out to be a temporary prison sentence – albeit that it was spread out over seven years. Today I think I must be the happiest man in the world. I certainly don't deserve to be where I am or to write books. But if you are unhappy with your job, I write as one who fully and rather deeply understands.

I would like to discuss the circumstances of unhappy employment, for various circumstances can lie behind this. For some, lack of education has meant that they will always be stuck in a certain kind of job. Let us say you are not going to be a doctor, a lawyer or an accountant, and what hurts is that there is a good possibility that you have a higher IQ than many of those who have had the education and got the good jobs. There are taxi drivers in London who have better minds than some lawyers. It hurts when you know you've got an ability. In the days when I sold vacuum cleaners I would go to church and hear some people preach, and it would almost drive me crazy. I didn't get edified when I went to church. Instead, I would think, 'These men can't preach their way out of a wet paper bag, and why am I not up there preaching? I am having to sit here listening and tomorrow morning I am going to have to go and knock on a door and say, "Hello, I am R.T. Kendall, I have come to show you something new and different for your home." ' I was stuck.

It could be that having qualifications means that you

don't get a job at all because your prospective employers consider you over-qualified. Or, if you do get a job, you accept a job that doesn't challenge you.

There are other things that may make your situation unhappy: having a boss, or the person just above you (whether it be headmaster, manager, supervisor), who is someone who revels in their position of power; having a boss who is not very bright, but blames everybody around them; having a boss who was promoted to the level of his or her incompetence. They shouldn't have that job, but you are having to listen and take orders and make that person happy. This is to say nothing of difficult people all around you who are selfish and insensitive, who are jealous of you, who needle you. Who lie about you, blame things on you. They will never admit, of course, that it is jealousy. That's the last thing we ever admit to about ourselves, so don't expect others to admit to it. Yet you can see why they are the way they are. On top of this, you are unappreciated. You don't get credit for hard work. You don't even get paid well. Some travel considerable distances to get just what work they can find. Then, after they get there, it is really dull. They dread arriving, they look forward to leaving, they look forward to Fridays and hate Mondays. On top of that they have to work hard, and inconvenient hours. In a word: lack of fulfilment. Sometimes the way they are treated is degrading. And as for a bit of prestige? It is out of the question. No prestige. But that was how it was for Joseph too.

But there is some compensation in unhappy employment. I don't refer to being paid a little extra or getting double pay for overtime. I am talking here about a different kind of compensation. The Bible says, 'The Lord was with Joseph.' Potiphar bought him from the Ishmaelites who had taken him to Egypt, but the Lord was with Joseph. I call that a wonderful compensation! Now if I can get this point across, it could change everything, and possibly give a person a different perspective. That is what I am hoping will happen as a result of this chapter.

Unhappy employment is *not* unusual. Tens of thousands will feel like you do tomorrow morning. You could go up and down the aisle of the train or the bus or the tube and say, 'Do you like your job? Are you happy?' and three out of four would probably say, 'No, I hate what I have to do!' So, you are not alone. Many are just like you, so what is unusual is *not* that you have unhappy employment. What *is* unusual is the fact that the Lord is with you: 'The LORD was with Joseph and he prospered, and he lived in the house of his Egyptian master' (Gen. 39:2).

What does it mean that the Lord was with him? It means that he had the presence of God. 'Keep your lives free from the love of money and be content with what you have, because God has said, "Never will I leave you; never will I forsake you." So we say with confidence, "The Lord is my helper; I will not be afraid. What can man do to me?" ' (Heb. 13:5–6).

One of the greatest things you can ever learn as a Christian is to remember that you have the presence of God. A verse that has meant the world to me is Psalm 16:8: 'I have set the LORD always before me. Because he is at my right hand, I shall not be shaken.' Why does it say he 'set the LORD' before himself? It means that he had to remind himself that the Lord was there. You see, setting the Lord before him didn't mean that by doing this the Lord managed to get there on time. No, the Lord was already there, because David went on to say, 'because he is at my right hand'. 'I have set the LORD' means he put himself in a frame of mind to *remind* himself that the Lord was already there. 'I have set the LORD always before me.' And if you can do this in the toughest moment, in the loneliest moment, then you know that he is there. Remind yourself, he is there. I wish I could explain how much comfort this gives me when I am praying. Sometimes when I am praying, I feel the Lord is not listening and I think, wait, hold it – Wow! He is listening and, in fact, he is right here; I remember Psalm 16:8, 'I have set the LORD always before me.' All of a sudden, I begin to feel him and it is so wonderful to know that he and the angels are watching. The presence of God. What compensation! The presence of God also means protection: 'You will not fear the terror of night, nor the arrow that flies by day, nor the pestilence that stalks in the darkness, nor the plague that destroys at midday. A thousand may fall at your side, ten thousand at your right hand, but it will not come near you' (Ps. 91:5–7).

What is unusual, then, is not that you have a job that you don't like. What *is* unusual is the fact that you have the Lord. Those people all around you, going into the City, wherever they go, probably don't have the Lord. But you do.

Eventually Joseph even prospered: 'The Lord was with Joseph and he prospered.' That doesn't mean that

Joseph made a lot of money as a servant but, as Stephen put it: 'Because the patriarchs were jealous of Joseph, they sold him as a slave into Egypt. But God was with him and rescued him from all his troubles. He gave Joseph wisdom and enabled him to gain the goodwill of Pharaoh king of Egypt; so he made him ruler over Egypt and all his palace' (Acts 7:9–10).

God even made it a little bit pleasant for Joseph as a servant. Potiphar put him in charge of his household and entrusted him with everything he owned. He began to see that the whole household was blessed because of Joseph. Even when I sold vacuum cleaners I made friends with some important people. The founder of Pepsi-Cola took me into his home and would come to see me. We've got a picture of him when he came to see us in his chauffeur-driven Cadillac. When my son T.R. was one, he gave him a big Pepsi-Cola bottle and a transistor radio. This important man would even ask me to pray for him! I never led him to Christ, but I tried. That is but one of many happy memories during the time I was out of the ministry, but locked into a humbling job. There were many compensations like that. If the Lord is with you, it should also make a difference in the office where you work, that things don't seem so bad.

Louise and I went to Russia in 1985, when it was the Soviet Union. We learned that there was a growing feeling among many, from the top down, that Christianity wasn't so bad after all. They found in every case, that if the worker was a Christian, they would get a good day's work out of them. If the employee was a Christian, then he or she didn't steal; they could be trusted.

Christians were soon getting promotions because they did such good jobs. What one can do is to be such a good employee, that you speak blessings to people. Don't be like so many Christians (forgive me) who are 'strange'. At work some people say, 'We know about her, she's a Christian and she sulks and sits in a corner.'

Arthur Blessitt, the man who has carried the cross around the world, has had a profound influence on us at Westminster Chapel. He has motivated us to talk to people about Jesus. I love the story he told about the lady who said, 'I don't ever tell people at work I am a Christian because I want my life to show.' One day somebody came to her after watching her for some time and said, 'You know, I have been watching you, you're different!' She began to think, 'It's paid off – thank you, Lord, I knew it would pay off one day.' She said, 'Yes, I am different.' 'Yes, I have been noticing you. I am going to ask you. Tell me, are you a vegetarian?'

If you are a Christian, then be nice. Speak blessings. Don't be unpleasant, bossy, always pointing the finger, especially if others know you are a Christian, which they should. There is a right way and a wrong way to witness. Don't witness on the job like we do on Saturdays on the streets. You don't go up to people and slap a Jesus sticker on them. But there is an intelligent way for people to know. You have what they don't have. God is with you.

There are of course complications with unhappy employment; nobody can deny this. Paul said, 'There was given me a thorn in the flesh, a messenger of Satan to torment me.' In what way is Satan responsible for unhappy employment? God gives the thorn, but allows

Satan to have a certain scope. The devil will use your weakness when you get alongside a certain type of person. There will always be one who gets your goat or who becomes a rival. Satan will work through a boss who is insensitive, uncaring and has no sense of God's honour. He will make you feel cheated in having a job in which you are unappreciated and unrecognised. The danger here for all of us is self-pity. The devil will exploit a situation through an immediate supervisor or the person near you who is less qualified than you, or one who is small-minded. In a word: he tries to make life miserable for you. The devil's purpose will be to try to create in you an attitude problem. If he can get you to have an attitude problem, then he's won, and the glory of God goes behind a cloud.

Therefore the devil works through your weakness when there are those around you who annoy you and are unkind. But you are the bigger person. You are the unusual one, for God is with you.

But that is not the only complication. Satan will put temptation in your way because you are already unhappy. Or if you are happy, he will still do this: put temptation in your way. It comes especially, though, to someone who feels that life is passing them by. You feel that you are missing out on life and Joseph could have said, 'What my brothers did wasn't right!' when temptation came his way. Here was a big test. Potiphar's wife began to flirt with Joseph. He could have said, 'Nobody will ever find out because she is not going to tell her husband, I don't know anybody in Egypt anyway, nobody in Caanan will ever find out, my dad will never find out.' He had the perfect cover, if you could call it that, for the affair. Yet he didn't start it. He could have said, 'She came to me, here I am, lonely, life is passing me by, I hate working here, I hate being in Egypt, I'll just have a little bit of fun.' But he said, 'No!' Had Joseph given in, it would have postponed what God might have done. Billy Graham has said it seems that the devil gets 75 per cent of God's best people through sexual temptation. Sexual sin brings incalculable damage to the kingdom of God. If Jim Bakker had not had the brief, fifteen-minute affair with Jessica Hahn, he wouldn't have gone to prison. But because he had the affair, his enemies all went for him and looked for ways to get at him.

This calls for conscientiousness in unhappy employment. Joseph said, 'I can't do this!':

But he refused. 'With me in charge,' he told her, 'my master does not concern himself with anything in the house; everything he owns he has entrusted to my care. No-one is greater in this house than I am. My master has withheld nothing from me except you, because you are his wife. How then could I do such a wicked thing and sin against God?' And though she spoke to Joseph day after day, he refused to go to bed with her or even be with her (Gen. 39:8–10).

Joseph was respectful of the one he worked for; he was conscientious. He also cared about God. Jesus said, 'He that is faithful in that which is least is faithful also in much' (Luke 16:10, AV). Joseph rose in a situation that was less than perfect, but all were blessed around him because of him. But sometimes such conscientiousness is not appreciated. Joseph was falsely accused and this became the biggest test.

Maybe you have been conscientious, you have been honest, you have done your best, but you have still been falsely accused. Well, sooner or later it happens to everybody who wants to do God's will:

> For it is commendable if a man bears up under the pain of unjust suffering because he is conscious of God. But how is it to your credit if you receive a beating for doing wrong and endure it? But if you suffer for doing good and you endure it, this is commendable before God. To this you were called, because Christ suffered for you, leaving you an example, that you should follow in his steps. 'He committed no sin, and no deceit was found in his mouth.' When they hurled their insults at him, he did not retaliate; when he suffered, he made no threats. Instead, he entrusted himself to him who judges justly (1 Pet. 2:19–23).

You may assume, because you have obeyed God, that he will clap his hands and say, 'That's wonderful, and just for that here's what I am going to do for you!' And you expect an immediate reward. Instead, as Luke 17:10 puts it: 'So you also, when you have done everything you were told to do, should say, 'We are unworthy servants; we have only done our duty.'' Therefore if you have done the right thing, but you are 'put in prison' for it, you can live with a good conscience because before God you have done the right thing.

The challenge of unhappy employment is a test from God. All the angels are watching. What will you do? Joseph was treated unjustly by his brothers, became a slave in a foreign country, had to do tasks for which he was not trained and, on top of it, was falsely accused. So what's the challenge? Make the best of a bad situation. Don't always run away to look for another job. Don't promote yourself to the level of your incompetence. Don't jump out of the frying pan into the fire. Remember that God put you there for a purpose. God could change everything overnight. Remember that this life is not all there is. Many around you don't have heaven to look forward to, and God doesn't want any of us to be *too* happy here below.

Unhappy employment may also help one to appreciate all the more the good things in one's life. It may be helpful and self-edifying to thank God for things that are positive. Do you have good health? Do you have a home? Do you have loved ones? Do you have friends you can share with? Do you also have a good relationship with God?

Your relationship with God is more important than your job. Get your joy from the inward anointing. There are some Christians who are happy with their jobs – so happy that they are not very spiritual. They don't pray, they don't have intimacy with God. With unhappy employment you may be enjoying a relationship with God that you might not otherwise have. God loves you and wants your company, and knows what you would be like if you were too comfortable.

We may or may not have it as bad as Joseph did; things

for him went from bad to worse. It was all part of his preparation. He had to learn to forgive his brothers, he had to forgive Potiphar's wife, he had to forgive Potiphar, he had to forgive God for all that God had permitted to happen; but he came out of it smelling like a rose, a changed man, devoid of bitterness.

The greater the suffering, the greater the anointing, and the greater your future. God will do this for you. It may not mean being Prime Minister, but you will reign one day and, when it comes, it will be worth waiting for. You will treasure that worst situation. Paul's thorn in the flesh was the best thing that could have happened to him.

4

An enemy

In this chapter we look at the possibility of one's thorn in the flesh being an enemy. There are those who believe that this was Paul's own thorn in the flesh. Paul had enemies, there's no doubt about that. Some think there may have been one enemy in particular who needled him and caused him pain. Some think it was the leader of the Judaisers, who I will explain below. Some think it was a leader of opposition at the church in Corinth. Some think it was Alexander the metalworker, to whom Paul refers in 2 Timothy 4:14.

We will not know until we get to heaven who or what Paul's thorn in the flesh was. As we have seen, Paul used the phrase as a metaphor. Not every Christian has an enemy as Paul had, but every Christian has a thorn in the flesh of some kind. If you say, 'I don't think I've got an enemy', then I must warn you that Jesus said, 'Woe to you when all men speak well of you, for that is how their fathers treated the false prophets' (Luke 6:26). You may be idling along comfortably, perhaps too comfortably. So God may look down from heaven and say, 'Well now, I think I know what I am going to have to do in your case.

I think you are too comfortable, I need to get your attention.' God can – overnight – raise up an enemy and that may work.

I don't think I really had an enemy until 1963 when Louise and I went to live in Carlisle, Ohio. The dispute was over the gospel, and someone in the church there tried to get rid of me. What happened was this. My old friend Billy Ball recommended me to a church that had this motto: 'No creed but Christ, no book but the Bible, no law but love'. That sounded pretty good to me. I was assured that if I preached from the Bible, they would accept it. I did, but they didn't. They had a creed indeed; my understanding of the Bible was foreign to them. They reported me to the authorities in their denomination. They tried me for 'heresy', charging me with preaching (1) Jesus is God; (2) Christians are still sinners, and (3) predestination. I pleaded guilty to all three, although they did not articulate any of them as I had done. The charges were dropped, but the members of my little church continued to intensify their opposition. I left soon afterwards.

But that was just a little bit of preparation for more to come. I have never had an enemy in the non-Christian world. Yet that fact doesn't cheer me up. All my enemies have been Christians. Sadly, Christians are not exempt from jealousy and ambition. I sometimes wonder how many theological controversies – past and present – are, in reality, theological issues. The untold story in so many famous accounts is that there was often a spirit of rivalry that was masked as being a theological issue. The truth will come out in the courtroom of God. Paul said when his teaching was being questioned:

> I care very little if I am judged by you or by any human court; indeed, I do not even judge myself. My conscience is clear, but that does not make me innocent. It is the Lord who judges me. Therefore judge nothing before the appointed time; wait till the Lord comes. He will bring to light what is hidden in darkness and will expose the motives of men's hearts. At that time each will receive his praise from God (1 Cor. 4:3–5).

What about you? Recently I heard a lovely quip from an Indian brother who is pastor of a Tamil church in East London:

> To dwell with the saints in heaven above,
> oh that will be glory.
> To dwell with the saints we know below,
> well that's another story!

Most of us are not prepared for where our enemy comes from. Diana, the late Princess of Wales, openly called the Royal Family 'the enemy'. However, we must be careful that the devil doesn't make someone appear as our enemy in case we unnecessarily alienate one who may in fact be a friend. Today's enemy could be tomorrow's friend. I hope and pray that I am nobody's enemy. There may be those who perceive me as the enemy, but I hope not. I don't want to be anyone's enemy, but there have been times when I have been keenly aware of an enemy.

I know that God has enemies. His enemy is the devil; the enemy of Jesus Christ is Satan. The enemy of the Holy Spirit is the devil, the enemy of the truth is the devil, the enemy of the Church is the devil, and God's enemies are those who are against the truth.

Be sure that you are in Christ. Be sure that you are covered by the blood of Jesus. Be sure that all your sins are under his blood, because you surely don't want God as an enemy. And yet even if you are saved and have been tip-toeing too near the world, I have to tell you, as James did, 'You adulterous people, don't you know that friendship with the world is hatred towards God? Anyone who chooses to be a friend of the world becomes an enemy of God' (Jas. 4:4). In other words, you can be saved, but God may seem like an enemy. For example, if you watch things on television that you know are not edifying you, participate in things you know are not good for your body, do that which you know does *not* draw you closer to God – and you do it deliberately – then God will seem like an enemy! You will wonder why things are happening, you will wonder why God is hiding his face. It is his way of getting your attention.

Be sure, then, that you know that your sins are forgiven, that you are walking in the light (1 John 1:7). You must not have God as your enemy. It's the worst position to be in – to have God against you. Jesus had his enemies. As far as I can tell, it was not from the Gentiles, it was from the religious people: the establishment, the Sanhedrin, the teachers of the Law, the Pharisees, the Chief Priests, the Sadducees.

Paul's enemies were undoubtedly Jews who hated him for confessing Jesus Christ as Messiah. The Judaisers that I referred to earlier were Jews who made professions of faith in Christ but hated Paul's gospel. Whether *that* was his thorn, we don't know, but clearly all of us have one enemy, the devil – and he hates us. He will work through people to bring us down.

The person Satan works through may be your own thorn in the flesh, but it is always God's way of getting your attention. Moses' enemy and the enemy of the ancient Israelites was Pharaoh: 'For the Scripture says to Pharaoh: "I raised you up for this very purpose, that I might display my power in you and that my name might be proclaimed in all the earth" ' (Rom. 9:17).

You may have a Pharaoh, or some kind of lesser enemy, a thorn in the flesh that needles you, gets your goat, agitates you, preoccupies your thoughts. David's enemy was King Saul, who became more worried about David than he was about the Philistines. Often, that can happen with Christians, even church leaders. They get more worried about somebody who is a threat to them than they are about the honour of God's name generally.

God may choose to get our attention and increase our anointing by the rival spirit of an enemy. Now a rivalry can be a friendly rivalry, but sometimes it can lead to hostility. A rival is a person who competes with you. If that rivalry becomes ever so slightly unfriendly – mark this down – then there will be a little bit of jealousy there. We can always see when the other person is jealous, but can we tell when we ourselves are jealous?

Ask yourself if an ingredient in this rivalry is not a little bit of jealousy. And yet a friendly rivalry can be healthy: 'As iron sharpens iron, so one man sharpens another' (Prov. 27:17). But if there is hatred in rivalry, there will probably be jealousy – maybe a lot.

There are many kinds of rivalry. Sometimes it is sibling rivalry; Jacob and Esau were rivals. There are brothers and sisters who don't speak to each other; it may go right back to childhood when a parent unwisely, sadly, preferred one child. Jealousy can be set up – as in the case of Jacob, who was responsible for the jealousy of his sons against Joseph. Sometimes money is involved and people fight over their inheritance. There can be a social rivalry, when people compete for prestige. Such people live to impress others by their material possessions or who they know. They want to impress by their job or their relationships and become the name-droppers of this world.

Then there is another kind of rivalry – when you have been made the underdog, but it should have been the other way around. For example, take Hannah, who became the mother of Samuel. She was loved by her husband, but he had another wife and the latter was the one who had the children. Hannah should have been the one who was blessed since she had her husband's love, but God raised up a rival. This pain drove Hannah to her knees. She prayed and fasted for a child, and God answered her prayer. Samuel began a new era of prophets and Israel was greatly blessed as a result. It was traceable to Hannah's rival.

> God moves in a mysterious way
> His wonders to perform;
> He plants His footsteps in the sea
> And rides upon the storm.
>
> (William Cowper)

Take the rivalry between Leah and Rachel. Rachel had the beauty and love of her husband, but Leah bore the children. This drove Rachel to her knees. 'Then God remembered Rachel; he listened to her and opened her womb. She became pregnant and gave birth to a son and said, "God has taken away my disgrace." She named him Joseph, and said, "May the Lord add to me another son" ' (Gen. 30:22–4).

The same was true in the case of Sarah. She had Abraham's love, but was barren. As Paul Cain says, 'Sometimes God strategically closes the womb of the church.' It is always for a greater purpose. Sarah suggested that Abraham sleep with her maidservant Hagar. The upshot was that Sarah became the underdog. Hagar conceived and she began to despise her mistress (Gen. 16:4). But that is not the end of the story, and Sarah later gave birth to Isaac. This inspired Isaiah to write:

> 'Sing, O barren woman,
>   you who never bore a child;
> burst into song, shout for joy,
>   you who were never in labour;
> because more are the children of the desolate woman
>   than of her who has a husband,'
> says the LORD (Isa. 54:1).

All this began with a rival; it advanced God's purpose. So with all of us; every rival in our lives may be seen as a thorn in the flesh to get us to pray harder.

There can also be a spiritual rivalry. Paul once stated it with a little bit of sarcasm: 'No doubt there have to be differences among you to show which of you have God's approval' (1 Cor. 11:19). There are always those who think they are more spiritual than anyone else. The issue sadly emerges: who is the more spiritual, who is God really with? 'He approves of me more than you!' God says, 'Really?' A rivalry is sometimes set up between two people who each suppose that they are the more spiritual, that they are in the right. This was going on in Philippi, when Paul said, 'I plead with Euodia and I plead with Syntyche to agree with each other in the Lord' (Phil. 4:2). Syntyche probably found a friend that she could talk to about Euodia and Euodia probably talked to her friends about Syntyche. God doesn't like this, but there is a purpose in it that can work for good.

There can be a strategic rivalry. Saul became jealous of David and David became the enemy of Saul for the rest of his life. It started when David had that wonderful victory over Goliath. But there were those who danced and sang, 'Saul has slain his thousands, and David his tens of thousands' (1 Sam. 18:8). It was insensitive of them to sing like that, but people do this sort of thing. Saul was very angry. This refrain galled him and from that time on 'Saul kept a jealous eye on David' (1 Sam. 18:9). David's hero became his enemy, but it was God's way of refining David's anointing – the best thing that could have happened to him. God uses an enemy to refine us. That is why it is strategic.

After David became king, his son Absalom stole the hearts of the people and became David's enemy (1 Sam. 15:4). It is always amazing where your enemies can come from. Do you have a rival? Does he or she compete with you for the approval of the people? Does somebody like this needle you? They know exactly how to upset you and they are convinced that their cause is just and right. You too have no doubt that your cause is just and right. Could this be your thorn in the flesh? Hopefully, it won't be a life sentence, but for the moment God has allowed a messenger of Satan to torment you.

I want to elaborate on this matter of the reason for the existence of an enemy. This is a point that we must never forget throughout this book. You will recall the twofold structure of the thorn in the flesh: the divine purpose and the demonic purpose. They are parallel; they emerge simultaneously. This is hard to understand, but God and the devil are equally at work. God's purpose is for our good; the devil's purpose is to torment us. God's strategy is designed so that we won't be conceited; the devil's strategy is to bring us down and to make us feel miserable.

Sometimes, though, having an enemy *is* avoidable, for an enemy can be of one's own making. We must ask ourselves this question: have we developed a pattern over the years of putting people's backs up? Does somebody near you say, 'I don't have any enemies, but you always seem to'? There always seems to be somebody. You have fallen out with this person, and then after a while there is another person. Ask yourself if this could be your fault. After all, some enemies are avoidable. Some of us always get people's backs up. Think about it.

On the other hand, the reason for having an enemy may be inevitable. You may be caught in the crossfire of ancient enemies. God put you where you are, but you suddenly become a target. Someone wants your job. Someone is jealous of your gift, your talent, your influence. It's a wicked world. If you are in a position of some influence and you are trying to live a godly life then the devil will attack you. He will likely work through a person who is jealous of you and who doesn't like it that you are where you are; this person will then look for something to criticise in you. I have always found that when people look for something in us, they will certainly find it. None of us is perfect, and Satan will attack in order to bring you down; it is not that you have done anything wrong – it's just that you are caught in the crossfire of a higher level of hostility.

What, then, is the good that God has in mind? The demonic purpose is to torment, but the divine purpose is for our refinement. The devil always overreaches himself. His attack ultimately serves to refine our anointing, as it did with David. And so with you – that's a promise!

As for refinement by the enemy, I can honestly say that having an enemy has always turned out to be the best thing that could have happened to me. One former deacon, who had to be excommunicated on a charge of schism, continued to attend the services. He always came with his notepad, looking for anything he might use against me. It kept me on my toes! It drove me much closer to God and helped me to refine my thinking more than ever. I certainly don't look forward to another attack or more hostile fire from an enemy, but I can say that if it comes, even though it may not be pleasant, I'll end up better off. It has always in the past turned out to be like that. I was all the better as a result.

Now that isn't the devil's purpose. The enemy's purpose is to bring us down so that we either give up or lose heart – or, better still, lose credibility. Your enemy doesn't want you to be admired. He will say anything that will cause more people to think less of you. That is what the devil wants. There is no doubt that people will think less of you because of things that will be said about you. But the fringe benefit, the blessing, for all of us – when people don't respect you as perhaps they once did – is wonderful. Speaking for myself, I wouldn't trade it for anything. If I had to make a choice, I would have it just as it is. I have always been all the better for any attack by an enemy. This is why God said to Pharaoh, 'I raised you up for this very purpose, that I might display my power in you and that my name might be proclaimed in all the earth' (Rom. 9:17). There is always a purpose. Joseph Tson used to say to me, 'God uses my enemies for his glory! They advance God's purpose in my life.' That is absolutely true.

When I first came to Westminster Chapel, I wouldn't have understood this. I recently preached in my old church, the Blue River Baptist Church in Salem, Indiana. They invited me there for a weekend meeting and one evening I spoke on 'What I have learned since I was your pastor', which was twenty-four years before. I then gave a list of things. At the top of the list was the teaching of total forgiveness. I explained that it was sad but true that I wouldn't have been able to preach in this way when I was at the Blue River Baptist Church in 1970–3. I have to say that I wouldn't have known about total forgiveness if I hadn't had an enemy, somebody who wanted to bring me down. It could originally have sunk me, but God sent Joseph Tson to me just in the nick of time. Joseph is one of the leading church leaders in Romania. I poured out my heart to him, hoping he would say, 'Get it out of your system – you have a right to be angry.' He said the opposite. 'R.T.', he said, 'you must totally forgive them!' It was the greatest word anybody has ever said to me.

Second on my list was my teaching on how to grieve, and how not to grieve, the Holy Spirit. I wouldn't know anything about this were it not for an enemy. Third on my list was refusing to vindicate oneself: I wouldn't have even known to think along these lines if it hadn't been for an enemy. This is to say nothing about how it has altered my sense of God, my communion with him, two-way communication, hearing his voice, knowing his will, feeling his presence.

If you have an enemy, don't resent it. Don't resent him – don't resent her! If you react with graciousness, if you respond with dignity, you may well treasure the scenario. You may even want to get a big picture of that person, enlarge it, frame it, and put it where you can see it every day and say, 'Thank God for him or her!' For the devil always overreaches himself. He is the instrument to torment. Paul himself reacted the right way. He said,

'That is why, for Christ's sake, I delight in weaknesses, in insults, in hardships, in persecutions, in difficulties. For when I am weak, then I am strong' (2 Cor. 12:10). Satan always goes too far, which means that he gets too optimistic since what he does backfires on him. The classic example of this is when the devil entered Judas Iscariot and Judas betrayed Jesus. Jesus was then crucified and the devil said, 'Look what I did! We got him! He's finished!' Jesus said, 'It is finished', and it turned out to be God's way of saving the world. That's the pattern, never forget it.

The word 'refinement' means when impurities and defects are removed. With every trial I have ever had it has turned out like this:

> The flame shall not hurt thee; I only design
> Thy dross to consume and thy gold to refine.

Have you a rival right now? Is there somebody bugging you? Is there somebody needling you? Is there somebody trying to get your goat – or have they already got your goat? If you think long and hard about this, and you dwell on it, it could destroy you. There's no guarantee that the devil *will* overreach himself if we become full of self-pity and develop a judgmental spirit. It is then that the devil will be saying, 'Oh it's working! It's working!' Don't let that happen.

God trusts us in letting us have an enemy: so that if we respond in the right way, we will be so much better off.

I have also learned that when there is an attack out of the blue, God knows I need it! Not that the accusation is necessarily fair. Often, it is a lie. It is wrong. It is false, but it hurts. But I say, 'Hey, I needed that!' Not because what they said was right or what they said was fair but because God wanted to refine something in me. Satan works through our enemies to defeat us, but if we react without grieving the Holy Spirit, then the result will be that it will refine us, not defeat us. There is a book I will never be able to write but I can give you the title: *My Enemies and How They Blessed Me*! One would think that the devil would learn a lesson. But when he comes along and finds us walking in the Spirit, it will backfire.

Satan stirred up Grecian widows in the early Church. They said, 'We are not getting our share' (see Acts 6:1–10), but God raised up deacons and there were more converted than ever. The Jews subsequently turned against Stephen; they killed him. But that led to the conversion of the greatest apostle of them all, Paul. The devil always goes too far if we respond in a way that doesn't grieve the Holy Spirit. The main way we grieve the Spirit is by being bitter and not forgiving those who have hurt us (Eph. 4:30ff).

But there is more, and I must mention this before I end this chapter: the possibility of reconciliation of an enemy. Has it occurred to you that God would want a reconciliation? The heart of God is reconciliation. God was in Christ reconciling the world to himself (2 Cor. 5:19). This is why Paul urged, 'I plead with you, Euodia, I plead with you, Syntyche, to agree with each other in the Lord.' He gives them equal attention, one at a time. Here are three principles:

First, if reconciliation is delayed and you know that this can't be helped – that there is no chance of a reconciliation at the moment – then be sure it's not your fault. Paul said, 'If it is possible, as far as it depends on you, live at peace with everyone' (Rom. 12:18). So if reconciliation is delayed, be sure that you are not the one causing the delay. Do everything that you can do to embrace that person.

Second, your enemy today might be your friend to-morrow. Be sure therefore that you show such love to that person now, for you may become friends later. You would want them to say to you, 'You were wonderful to me during that time.' That means that while they are not wanting to be your friend, you never say a word about them to anybody, not a word. This will make it easier for you to become friends one day. That way, nobody will walk up to you and say, 'Oh, I see you two are speaking now', for it would show that somebody blabbed every-thing. Let the other person say what they want about you, while you behave yourself brilliantly. When there is a reconciliation they can say, 'You were great, you were great!' In the meantime don't let them be intimidated by you. If you get a good feeling when another person is just a little bit afraid of you, you are in the wrong. It shows a bad spirit. God isn't like that. Jesus isn't like that. People felt comfortable around Jesus. Let your enemy just feel at home with you. You may say, 'Well, that's asking a lot!' Yes. It's the standard of Jesus. Listen to this: 'If you love those who love you, what credit is that to you? Even "sinners" love those who love them' (Luke 6:32). Jesus says, give, lend to those from whom you don't expect to get anything in return, and just love them. Love them! That will make all the difference.

The third principle is this. Pray for your enemy. How do you pray for them? You must not pray that God will deal with them or punish them, but you must pray for them to be blessed: 'But I tell you who hear me: Love your enemies, do good to those who hate you, bless those who curse you, pray for those who ill-treat you. . . . If you love those who love you, what credit is that to you? Even "sinners" love those who love them. . . . Be merciful, just as your Father is merciful' (Luke 6:27–8, 32, 36).

When Jesus was on the cross and the people were mocking him, he might have said, 'I forgive you because you don't know what you are doing', but Jesus went right to the root. He said, 'Father, you forgive them.' This is why Jesus told us to pray for our enemies. You might say, 'That means that they are going to get away with it!' Could be. What if they do? 'Well, that's not right,' you say. Life isn't fair, but wait a minute. Are you so good and godly and pious and perfect that you haven't wanted to get away with something? And if you say, 'But I haven't been as bad as they have been,' do you know what God may do to you? He may just let you fall. I mean fall into sin – big time – show you what you are. Because Jesus said, 'Do not judge, or you too will be judged' (Matt. 7:1). Once you start judging, God may say, 'Hmm, you don't know what your heart is capable of, do you?' He may just withhold restraining grace and let you slip, and do for you that which you thought you could never do – shut your mouth.

The truth is, we have all got away with a lot. We all have skeletons in the cupboard. God has been gracious to all of us. So pray for your enemy. I repeat: don't pray that God deal with them! Say, 'God forgive them!' That means God releases them. That means that you are telling God that he doesn't have to deal with them, only forgive them and let them go! Then add: 'Forgive me for the way I feel about that person.' Prove that you really do mean this by employing the following principles: (1) Let nobody know what that person has done to you. (2) Don't allow the person to be intimidated or afraid of you. (3) Don't let the person feel guilty. (4) Let the person save face. (5) Protect that person from their deepest fear. This is the way Joseph forgave his brothers (Gen. 45:1–15).

When you have begun to pray like this, you are there. God will look down and say, 'Very good!' He may remove the thorn, but if he hasn't removed it, it's because you still need it.

One day all will be revealed: 'Therefore judge nothing before the appointed time; wait till the Lord comes. He will bring to light what is hidden in darkness and will expose the motives of men's hearts. At that time each will receive his praise from God' (1 Cor. 4:5). That will happen. We will know who was right, whether we have truly forgiven and prayed for our enemies (Mark 11:25). And after you have done everything, as long as the Holy Spirit in you is ungrieved, that very enemy will turn out to be the reason you began to grow by leaps and bounds and began to love, and to experience unusual power. You will thank God for that thorn in the flesh that would not go away.

5

A handicap or disability

We have seen in this book that Paul uses the term 'thorn in the flesh' as being both theological and metaphorical. By theological he refers to God's purpose in sending the thorn. It is to keep him humbled. By saying that it is a thorn in the flesh he refers to his fallen nature, with particular reference to his pride. It means that sanctification is something God takes seriously. Because none of us by nature really wants to be holy, we will seek the honour that comes from one another rather than the honour that comes from God only (John 5:44). None of us would aspire to seek the face of God on our own. Our hearts are deceitful, our fallen nature is always there.

> Prone to wander, Lord, I feel it,
> Prone to leave the God I love.

So the apostle Paul admitted that he needed his thorn in the flesh. It was, as we have seen, a *severe* form of chastening. Chastening or disciplining, when God teaches us a lesson and enforces us to learn, so that we may share in his holiness.

We have also seen that the phrase 'thorn in the flesh' is a metaphorical expression, used in such a general way that we can all identify with it. I repeat, every sovereign vessel has a thorn in the flesh. What may be mine may not be yours, what may be yours may not be mine. God knows our frame. He knows what each of us needs. He knows how to get our attention, each one of us. To determine what Paul's thorn actually was, is an unprofitable exercise.

Anyone's thorn is a 'handicap', or disability, in a sense. Nowadays we use the term 'disabled' of someone who has some kind of physical, emotional or mental limitation. But I am also using the term 'handicapped' as well, since it is an umbrella term that covers more than one kind of disability. We all have a 'handicap' of some sort, and there is a sense in which every subject in this book could be called a 'handicap'. But there are those who have a more severe kind of handicap and that's what we are going to look at in this chapter.

A 'handicap' is any nuisance that hinders progress, success or happiness. It is an inconvenience that is likely to be permanent. As I said above, it's like a prison sentence: you are locked into a situation or condition that is likely to be around for a while. But remember that the thorn in the flesh is given sovereignly by God – that is, by his sovereign permission. It is carried out by the devil, but – paradoxical as it may seem – God gives it. Paul said, 'A messenger of Satan came to torment me.'

Now why is this chapter so important? It is to show more clearly the purpose of a thorn in the flesh. It is also to encourage all of us with some disability to know exactly how we are to accept it. It is important to understand those who may have a much more difficult handicap than our own.

A few years ago my wife started a ministry to the deaf in Westminster Chapel. This came about because when on holiday Louise had punctured her eardrum and developed tinnitus which affected her hearing. Soon after we got back to Westminster Chapel she happened to meet Judith Brittain, a deaf lady who is a sign language teacher. At that very moment Louise felt a strong impulse to learn sign language, having some idea of what it is like not to hear well. The end result today is a flourishing ministry to deaf people in Westminster Chapel – just another token of how God uses a trauma in one's life. 'Sweet are the uses of adversity,' wrote Shakespeare. We have also learned many things about deafness generally, and deaf people in particular, that we did not previously know. And we are still learning. For one thing, we are dealing with a rather different culture. Despite frustrations and a need for great patience with the hearing community, one rarely finds self-pity among the deaf.

It shows that when we come to terms with what our own handicap or disability is, we see that we are so much better off than others. This should also help us to understand those who may have a different handicap from our own.

Perhaps the main thing to remember, though, is that self-pity is to be avoided. Why? God takes the responsibility for sending the 'thorn' but self-pity becomes sin against God and – whatever our handicap may be – we must keep in mind it is from God and for our good. It is only a matter of time before we may learn to be thankful for it.

Andrew Griffin, a quadriplegic member of our church, knowing that I was preparing this chapter, sent me a note:

Many people have a thorn in their flesh from their mother's womb. God gives us the thorn not to forget about him. That's what happened to my mother when I was born thirty-eight years ago. My life when I was a teenager was hard enough. I rejected God. I hit rock bottom. It wasn't until I was twenty-seven years old that I went to Cheltenham to a college for the handicapped and the thorn in the flesh led me to God. I was baptised in the Baptist Church in Cheltenham, and I became a Christian Union leader. I went to see Billy Graham in Gloucester, and from there I went from strength to strength. The power of God was always at my heart from then. I got my own flat in London, and I went to Westminster Chapel. I heard about forgiveness of the spirit . . . and I went forward. From that day, I was focused on my college in West London. My grades improved, my concentration has got stronger. I have computer examinations, English qualifications, business qualifications and I have succeeded in all of them. Now I am on a junior access course. I am hoping to go on to a

main access and then to university. There is a
lesson about this. Jesus had a cross to bear and
we have to learn from that.

Andy fears that most people don't understand disabled
people; for one thing, people patronise them – treat them
as abnormal. Andy wrote this partly to stress that a
disabled person is normal. What often happens is that
someone goes up to a disabled person, notices the person
next to them, does not even look at the disabled person,
but says to the friend, 'How is he today?' And the
disabled person is right there, aware of this! 'You could
have asked me,' he wants to say.

A person may go up to someone who is deaf and, even
though many deaf people can lip-read, will disregard that
and not treat the person with dignity. I remember when
we used to go out and eat with Orion Osburn, a friend
who is blind. We would order; he would order. The
waiter or waitress would say to me, 'How does he want
his steak cooked?' He would say, 'Just because I'm blind,
it doesn't mean I can't speak for myself!' Sadly many
people still don't treat handicapped people as normal
people.

We all have abilities for which we can be thankful. I
wonder, how often do we thank God? 'Lord, I thank
you that I've got eyes, that I've got ears, that I've got the
use of my limbs.' We could go on and on. I don't mean
to sound harsh, but God does not like ingratitude. He
doesn't like it one bit. For those of us who take him for
granted, and we are all guilty of this, let us start now to
thank him for all we have.

Jesus put it this way:

> When you give a luncheon or dinner, do not
> invite your friends, your brothers or relatives, or
> your rich neighbours; if you do, they may invite
> you back and so you will be repaid. But when
> you give a banquet, invite the poor, the crippled,
> the lame, the blind, and you will be blessed.
> Although they cannot repay you, you will be
> repaid at the resurrection of the righteous. (Luke
> 14:12–14).

I would think that a great sign of God's approval and
anointing on any church is to see it filled with people in
wheelchairs; for it to be filled with deaf and blind people.
The reason is because such people obviously feel welcome. The word gets out that this church wants and
needs the disabled. They know they will be treated with
dignity and respect. People everywhere want to spend
time with them; they will come and talk to them!

Do you do that at your church? Or do you hurry to be
with the people you already know? I really want this
chapter to have an effect on every reader. God wants his
Church to include everybody. It's not just the pain,
difficulty or the inconvenience; the real problem is the
way disabled people are marginalised and put to one side.

There is more than one kind of handicap and there are
obviously various degrees of being disabled. There are
generally two kinds of disabled people: those who are
born disabled, and those whose handicap affects them
later in life. The blind man in John 9 had been blind from
birth: 'As he went along, he saw a man blind from birth.

His disciples asked him, "Rabbi, who sinned, this man or his parents, that he was born blind?" "Neither this man nor his parents sinned," said Jesus, "but this happened so that the work of God might be displayed in his life" ' (John 9:1–3). Some are born blind, some are born deaf, and some are crippled from birth (Acts 3:2).

Others become disabled through illness. This can happen to any of us. It can happen through an accident, or it may be the gradual loss of our hearing or sight. The loss of the use of limbs can be anyone's experience.

But there is another kind of handicap, mental impairment, those born with mental limitations. It may be a low IQ, or those born with Down's syndrome. There are those who have a learning disability, like dyslexia. Some lose the ability to think clearly. It may come from an accident, from an operation, or from senility – perhaps, Alzheimer's disease.

Another kind of handicap is to be emotionally disturbed. It may come from a deprived childhood, from lack of security. Or it may come from a trauma, because of an abuse that left a severe impairment of the emotions. The result could be depression or a sexual misgiving. It may be an inability to live in the real world. Such people often love the Lord Jesus Christ with deepest devotion, but wonder what's wrong with them. And yet God allows this because he has a purpose in it all. He loves us so much, and what is often seen as a negative in this life will be seen in the opposite way when we get to heaven.

There are other kinds of handicaps in today's society. Think of those of us who are the objects of racial prejudice. All because of the colour of our skin! There are countless millions who are misjudged and put to one side because of their ethnic or educational background. Take a country where there is a class system and you are at the bottom! What a handicap! Consider a class society in which one's accent immediately disqualifies that person for a job. Do you have any idea how hard it is for some of the best people with the brightest minds who cannot get a good job? It becomes a very real handicap and it is only because people are prejudiced.

We can all find some handicap in our lives, but how many are *truly* disabled and hurting? I address such now, you who are disabled. I want to deal with the nuisance of being handicapped or disabled. I only wish you could feel that the Holy Spirit is directing my words in such a way that you say, 'Oh, I can see that God knows. God knows. People may not know. God knows and God understands.' There is the perpetual nuisance of disability. I think of Mephibosheth (2 Sam. 9:1–13). We are told that Jonathan, the son of Saul, had a son who was lame in both feet. His nurse had hurriedly picked him up; he fell and became crippled. He lived with this disability for the rest of his life. But King David was gracious to him and invited him to sit at the King's table for life. But David later fled into exile. When David later returned home, his first question was: 'What has happened to Mephibosheth?' Sadly, Mephibosheth was lied about. It was said that Mephibosheth betrayed David. The truth was the opposite. It's just another example of how a disabled person can be misunderstood. People do not realise the inconvenience and loss. A deaf person cannot speak on the telephone. A deaf person cannot answer the door without aid of some kind. The blind cannot watch television or see what people look like. They never see a sunrise or sunset. Some of those in wheelchairs cannot wash or dress themselves.

One friend of ours, who was a faithful member of our Thursday lunchtime congregation, a solicitor at Scotland Yard, asked us to pray about a small tumour on his back. We prayed for it, but it got worse. The doctors said that he would have to have an operation or he would become paralysed. He had the operation, but became paralysed anyway. It got steadily worse and now he is in a wheel-chair. He has to get up at 5 o'clock every day just to wash and dress to be able to leave for work at 7 o'clock.

I think of Joni Eareckson Tada. She can never dress herself. She has to be carried to bed. She must be spoon-fed. Think of the humbling – dare I call it, humiliation – of having to be waited on, feeling constantly patronised.

There is the nuisance of isolation. Unless people learn sign language, or a deaf person is very good at lip-reading, that deaf person is not likely to be invited to a hearing person's home for a meal. Can you imagine the lack of fellowship this results in? Many deaf people do not realise their full job potential, which can be very frustrating.

Then there is the matter of a sense of personal identity, because disabled people are often robbed of dignity by the people who consciously or unconsciously isolate them. However, when you are a Christian, and you see this as a thing that God has allowed, you develop your own sense of dignity, get your positive self-image from the way God sees you. Yet when such people are robbed of dignity, it must be the toughest thing of all to rise above the daily nuisance of wondering whether you are loved. The eyes of the people will not often help. Such people get their identity from God, from Jesus, even though they may seem like invisible people when it comes to the eyes of the world.

If you are a disabled person, where do you get your strength? I think one must begin with accepting oneself. You accept your handicap or disability, whatever it is. You must see it as a manifestation of God's glory. Clearly, it would not be your own choice as to how God manifests his glory, but you accept it. You accept it as his will. I promise this: as you accept it as being from God, then the day will come – for many, it already has – when you truly thank him for it.

Whatever your handicap or disability is, if you accept it as being from God, it is only a matter of time until you see a purpose for good in it. Take it from God with both hands. Why? Because he loves you and it was his inscrutable, sovereign way of getting you to develop intimacy with him.

All of us, including people with disabilities, need an opportunity to off-load and share frustrations. But this should be without complaining. There must be no self-pity. Perhaps you have complained. Who hasn't? We all have. But where do we go from here? I would only say this: if up to now you have complained, then confess it to God (1 John 1:9). Can you pray the following prayer?

I am sorry. I am sorry for complaining about this handicap in my life. I can see that you have done it. And if you have done it, that makes it right. And even though now I don't understand the reason, I am going to give you the benefit of the doubt and I know that one day I will see the reason.

I would urge you, whatever you are going through, whatever robs you of the happiness you desire, to know that God has allowed this for a purpose. Accept it. Accept it as being from a loving God. Then accept it in this way: come to terms with it. Don't pretend it's not there. Admit that it probably won't go away – at least, not for a while. God could remove it, yes, just like that! But, apart from divine intervention, come to terms with the likely fact that it is there to stay.

Acceptance therefore means you don't deny it. There will be no repressing; don't live in denial – pretending it's not there. God has allowed it and it is there to stay. How do you get your nourishment, your strength? Accept your handicap or disability.

But there is more. Know that God loves you. Most important of all, know that you are saved. The greatest thing in the world is knowing that you will go to heaven when you die. For there are people with no handicap, no disability, who have everything in this life, but when they die they will not go to heaven. There are also handicapped and disabled people who are not saved. There is only one reason you are saved: that God was good to you. He gave you the gospel, and never forget that this life is not all there is. We are on our way to face God at the judgment. Life at its longest is still short. It will soon be over. What happens when you die? It is either heaven or hell. To know that you are going to go to heaven, that you are saved and that God loves you, is the greatest thing of all.

Also know that you must be special, because you are. God doesn't give this particular thorn in the flesh to everybody. The big thing that has burned on me as I have prepared this important chapter is: in heaven you will see how blessed you were on earth to have had the privilege of this disability. It may not seem that way now. But I can tell you that if there is anything that has been clear to me, it is this. We will be eternally grateful in heaven for our particular thorn. For there is a definite, thought-out reason why God has done this. It is to drive us closer to him, not further from him. It is to keep us from being smug, conceited or taking ourselves too seriously. God *could* step in and take it away. But if he doesn't, it will stay only because God's purpose in it all is still unfulfilled.

Although I wish with all my heart that God would remove my own 'thorn in the flesh', I have to say also that I have become reconciled to its permanence. What I never thought I would say to God, I now find myself praying: 'Lord, I believe now that it would be wrong if you took my thorn away.' I can now see that it has been so essential to all that I have done. I have stopped praying that it will go, because I think it is one of the best things that ever happened to me. I would therefore urge you, if you are waking up each morning and saying, 'It's still here, it's still here', to admit that, though you want it removed, there is a wider purpose in it all that God alone understands:

Delight yourself in the LORD and he will give
you the desires of your heart (Ps. 37:4).

For the LORD God is a sun and shield; the
LORD bestows favour and honour; no good thing
does he withhold from those whose walk is
blameless (Ps. 84:11).

'For my thoughts are not your thoughts,
neither are your ways my ways,' declares the
LORD. 'As the heavens are higher than the earth,
so are my ways higher than your ways and my
thoughts than your thoughts' (Isa. 55:8–9).

Whatever our thorn in the flesh is, and regardless of
whether we have asked for it to be removed (as we surely
have), I urge all of us to realise that it is there because God
says it is still right for it to be there. One day you will see;
God did it just for you.

You also need anticipation. Yes! Anticipation that
God will heal. Never give up hope. It is true that
God will use you all the more and all the better because
that disability is still there. I asked Joni Eareckson Tada,
'Would you like to be healed?' I thought she would have
a quick answer, because I thought everyone asked her
that. But it was as though she had never even thought
about it! Finally she said, 'Yes, yes, yes, but,' she continued, 'the most precious time of my day is when they
put me to bed and I am just alone with the Lord. I am so
afraid that if I didn't have this paralysis, I wouldn't have
that intimacy.' But never abandon the anticipation that
God will step in and heal you, as he did with Jennifer

Rees-Larcombe. She never gave up hope. Neither should you.

The reward for being patient and not complaining is worth waiting for. It is what helps ensure a great reward when you get to heaven. In my opinion, because of the nature of this kind of affliction, when one doesn't complain, the reward will be far, far greater. I say to anybody in a wheelchair, to anybody who is deaf or blind, or whatever the impairment is, you have an opportunity to have a most dazzling reward in heaven. Because of the nature of your kind of affliction, if there is no self-pity, the reward will be far, far greater than that of others. It will be certainly greater than it would have been had you not had it. The greater the affliction, the greater the reward. The greater the suffering, the greater the anointing. All this is guaranteed if you and I don't give in to self-pity or complaining.

Fanny J. Crosby was blind from birth. She never saw a sunset, never saw a flower, but wrote many hymns, including 'Blessed Assurance', 'All the Way My Saviour Leads Me' and 'I Will See Him Face to Face'. Someone once said to her, 'Miss Crosby, I feel so sorry for you; you've never seen a flower, you've never seen the faces of people around you.' 'Oh,' she said, 'you feel sorry for me? Don't you know that the first face I will get to see will be the face of Jesus?' As someone else put it:

> It will be worth it all when we see Jesus,
> Life's trials will seem so small when we see him.

The thorn in the flesh gives one the possibility of a

greater reward than we would have had. The greater the handicap, the greater the impairment, the greater the disability, the greater the reward if we don't murmur. Here below you may have felt it was a deprivation. In heaven you will say, if I dare use this word, 'How *lucky* I was to have it.' I guarantee that this is the case.

6

Unhappy living conditions

Have you ever thought of your own thorn in the flesh as your having to live in a place that makes you unhappy? We all have to live somewhere until we die and, for many, it is a case of very unhappy living conditions. As for Paul's own thorn in the flesh, I can only reiterate that we will not know what his was until we get to heaven. But he has given us this figure of speech, which we can all identify with. If you are saved and have been chosen for a special task, I can tell you that you have got a thorn in the flesh of one sort or another.

Unhappy living conditions might have been Paul's thorn, because he let us know that being an apostle was the opposite of luxury. I think of a lot of big-name preachers today who live in luxury. As someone once put it, when Paul came to town, he said, 'Where's the best jail?' Today, church leaders go into town and say, 'Where's the best hotel?' Paul said:

> For it seems to me that God has put us apostles
> on display at the end of the procession, like men
> condemned to die in the arena. We have been

made a spectacle to the whole universe, to angels as well as to men. We are fools for Christ, but you are so wise in Christ! We are weak, but you are strong! You are honoured, we are dishonoured! To this very hour we go hungry and thirsty, we are in rags, we are brutally treated, we are homeless. We work hard with our own hands. When we are cursed, we bless; when we are persecuted, we endure it; when we are slandered, we answer kindly. Up to this moment we have become the scum of the earth, the refuse of the world (1 Cor. 4:9–13).

The Authorised Version says, 'no certain dwelling place' in 1 Corinthians 4:11; the New International Version translates it as 'homeless'. Jesus said, 'Foxes have holes and birds of the air have nests, but the Son of Man has no place to lay his head' (Luke 9:58). There will be those reading this book for whom this is your very problem; and there will also be those for whom this is certainly *not* your problem. Your home is your castle. You've got warmth, you've got comfort, and you cannot complain. I would have to say that this is not my thorn in the flesh. I do know what it is to have the opposite, but in recent years God has been so good to us. How many of us take time to thank God that we are comfortable?

But I am thinking in this chapter of those who are stuck. You may be living in a country or area you would not have chosen. Perhaps you are from the north of England and you have to live in the south. Maybe you are from Wales and you have to live in England. Or you love the country, yet have to live in the city; it's the only place where you can get a job. You have no choice at the moment.

I want to say to you that this is from God, for this may well be your thorn in the flesh. I write these lines that you will come to terms with what God has done and accept that it is for you at the moment. Can you do that? Having to cope with bad neighbours. Having to cope with strange people, noisy rude people who love, it seems, to make life miserable for you. There are people like that.

I know a man who said that the neighbours kept the television on loud night after night and, when he could take it no longer, he complained to them, and they called the police out to question him! There are some strange people out there, and perhaps you live in a situation like this.

Some are surrounded by anti-God neighbours, even those who are involved in the occult. This gives you a strange feeling. Have you ever thought of praying for the sprinkling of the blood of Jesus on your very premises? I would urge you to do that. Go into every room, and perhaps bring someone else with you to pray that the blood of Jesus will be, as it were, a covering over where you live.

For some, their environment is unsafe. There is the constant fear of a break-in. You are worried about being mugged the moment you walk outside. You worry as you come home that you may have been burgled.

Some live in very small quarters, a tiny room. For some, their flat or house is always cold and damp, or the plumbing doesn't work. Some have to climb several flights of stairs as there is no lift; others live where there is a lift but it always smells of urine. But that is where you have to live. There are those who have no convenient facilities and the appliances are out of date. You may be preoccupied with how it is when you have to go to that place you dread to call 'home', and you hate having to call it 'home'. On top of that, some have to live alone. You not only have what I wrote about in a previous chapter – loneliness – but it is compounded by unhappy living conditions.

Some have to live with people who won't allow them any privacy. Perhaps you are stuck with difficult family members. There will always be those who play the television too loud, or control which channel it's on, or won't keep the place clean; a place where there is no real fellowship, and no way you can enjoy a little blissful solitude. There are also those who live rough. Some choose that, but others don't.

Are you aware that there is a sense in which a main issue in both the Old Testament and the New Testament has to do with living conditions? The Old Testament stresses again and again the matter of living conditions. Moses and the people of Israel lived in a desert, and they were looking for a land flowing with milk and honey. The thrust of the Law was: if you obey, certain happy living conditions will follow. If you disobey, the opposite will follow (see Deut. 28:1–61). In the New Testament, sadly, the Jews' messianic expectations had to do entirely with living conditions. They thought that when Messiah came, he was going to change living conditions for them and set them free from Rome. This is why they couldn't cope with the thought that their Messiah would end up on a cross. Jesus warned them, for he knew exactly what they were thinking. He said in Luke 17:20–1, 'The kingdom of God does not come visibly, nor will people say, "Here it is," or "There it is," because the kingdom of God is within you.' Jesus put it like that so that they would understand that this present world is not all there is.

For some people, their only reward is in this present life. I read recently about ten individuals who have been chosen to be commemorated in Westminster Abbey. That would mean everything for some – the ultimate goal. I have never ceased to be amazed by those who just want their name to be carved in history so that, down the line, people will remember their name. Whatever will that mean when we get on the other side and find what really has value? Paul said, 'For the kingdom of God is not a matter of eating and drinking, but of righteousness, peace and joy in the Holy Spirit' (Rom. 14:17).

In this chapter I want to examine two eras, one of the patriarchs and the other of Moses. Both had the call of God on them, and both experienced unhappy living conditions. In the case of Abraham, he did not know in advance the lifestyle to which he would be called: 'By faith Abraham, when called to go to a place he would later receive as his inheritance, obeyed and went, even though he did not know where he was going' (Heb. 11:8). Here was a person who had the call of God upon him. As for living conditions, he made his home in the promised land like a stranger in a foreign country and 'lived in tents' (Heb. 11:9). How would you like to live for years and years in a tent? But could not this also have been part of the secret of his great anointing? It was also said of Moses, 'By faith Moses, when he had grown up, refused to be known as the son of Pharaoh's daughter' (Heb. 11:24).

Here was a man brought up in a palace who 'chose to be mistreated along with the people of God rather than enjoy the pleasures of sin for a short time' (Heb. 11:25). Can you imagine someone who lived in Buckingham Palace or Windsor Castle and who gave it up voluntarily in order to please God? Don't tell me this had nothing to do with Moses' anointing! I say it had everything to do with it.

The call of God on a person makes all the difference. Why did Moses do what he did? Why was Abraham enabled and motivated to go into a strange country? It is because the call of God is paramount.

Is the call of God upon you? Is your motivating sense of life the call of God? If you say, 'Well, I am not sure if it is or not', you ought to fall on your face before God and ask, 'What has gone wrong? What has happened?' Do you have no sense of destiny? No reason for living? Have you gone off the rails to such an extent that there is no sense of the call of God on you?

You may hope that living conditions will change and this will give you a little bit of happiness. But the most important thing is to know that God's call is on you. There is something for every one of us to do that is as important in our sphere as in any others, in world history! As St Augustine put it, 'God loves every man or woman as though there were no one else to love.' Every Christian has a call from God, and when that grips you and you know that God has a plan for your life, you will see everything else in a different light, including where you live.

But having felt the call, one makes a choice. What was Abraham's choice? It was to obey. Consider it again: 'By faith Abraham, when called to go to a place he would later receive as his inheritance, obeyed and went, even though he did not know where he was going' (Heb. 11:8). Abraham had to make a choice. The call of God was on him, and did he accept it? Abraham had a nephew by the name of Lot. The two of them reached a place so that each of them had to make a choice: 'So Abram said to Lot, "Let's not have any quarrelling between you and me, or between your herdsmen and mine, for we are brothers. Is not the whole land before you? Let's part company. If you go to the left, I'll go to the right; if you go to the right, I'll go to the left" ' (Gen. 13:8–9).

This is because things just didn't matter that much to Abraham! He said, 'Make a choice, I'll just go one way, it doesn't matter to me.' Why? He had obeyed. A sense of destiny was on him; that is what kept him going. He knew that everything was not to be understood in terms of material things. Sadly, do you know what it says about Lot? It says, 'Abram lived in the land of Canaan, while Lot lived among the cities of the plain and pitched his tents near Sodom. Now the men of Sodom were wicked and were sinning greatly against the LORD' (Gen. 13:12–13). That was a bad choice.

Sometimes there is something you can do about this

matter of living conditions. They may be what they are because of a bad choice. As to how you know whether you should be doing something about changing your living conditions instead of just putting up with them, the answer is twofold. First, has God unmistakably put you where you are? If so, you should stay there for the time being. He has a purpose in it for you. Secondly, if your being where you are is because of a hasty decision – and you've had no peace since – I would suggest God has a better plan for you. Pray that God will move you without you 'jumping out of the frying pan into the fire'. Consider Paul's words: 'Let us therefore make every effort to do what leads to peace and to mutual edification' (Rom. 14:19). When you have true peace within you are probably doing what is right; if you lose that peace you are – for the moment – not where you should be.

Lot pitched his tent towards Sodom when he knew that this was edging as near to the world and temptation as he could get. There are those who fancy that they are strong enough, that they can live right next to the world. It doesn't seem to matter who their friends are. 'I am strong enough,' they say. The next thing we know is that Lot got into real trouble. Could it be that you have chosen to live too close to the world, as close as you could get, and now you are having to pay for this choice? The day came when Lot had two angels visit him. The men in the town square heard about these two visitors. They went to Lot and nearly broke the door down. 'They called to Lot, "Where are the men who came to you tonight? Bring them out to us so that we can have sex with them" ' (Gen. 19:5). Lot says, 'Oh no, my friends. Don't do this wicked thing.' He said, 'Look, I have two daughters who have never slept with a man. Let me bring them out to you, and you can do what you like with them. But don't do anything to these men, for they have come under the protection of my roof' (Gen. 19:8).

Who would have thought that a father of his own children would sink so low? If you had asked Lot back when he pitched his tent towards Sodom, 'Do you think you will ever stoop so low as to do a thing like that?' he would have said, 'No!' He would have found this horrifying! Likewise there are those suffering the consequence of a choice once made, who have done things of which they once said, 'Oh, I'll never do that!' And they have done just that! Yet the interesting thing is, Peter calls Lot a righteous man (2 Pet. 2:7). The Authorised Version refers to 'just Lot'. In fact, Peter also said that the Lord knows how to deliver the godly from trials (2 Pet. 2:9).

Lot was spared because he was the Lord's. I trust that his daughters survived their father's insensitivity as well. But he almost got burned. Could it be that God brought you to this place of crisis at this moment? Things can change. You may be living with the consequences of a bad choice, but it is a new day and I would not write like this if there were no hope. Your life may not have to stay as it is. Something can happen in your heart before God, and you can say 'I am sorry, I am sorry!' and know that God loves you as much as he loved Lot and Abraham.

Moses' choice was quite amazing: 'He regarded disgrace for the sake of Christ as of greater value than the treasures of Egypt, because he was looking ahead to his reward' (Heb. 11:26). The call of God was on him, and he too made a choice; but I don't think Moses had a clue how bad it would really get. I don't think many missionaries, when they accept the call to go to an alien country, know what they are letting themselves in for. Sometimes God motivates us just a little bit at a time and then down the road we think, 'Oh, I didn't know it would lead to this!' Moses could not have known how bad things would be, but he made a choice. Once we make the choice, there is no turning back, and Moses' choice was to be mistreated with God's people as opposed to enjoying the pleasures of sin. It is interesting that it says, 'the pleasures of sin for a short time'. They don't last long. The 'fun' passes so quickly, and one looks back and says, 'It wasn't worth it!'

We come now to the heart of the matter: living conditions. 'By faith he made his home in the promised land like a stranger in a foreign country; he lived in tents, as did Isaac and Jacob, who were heirs with him of the same promise' (Heb. 11:9). Isn't that something? He made his 'home' in a foreign land, yet he was a stranger. The word 'home' is one of the most beautiful words in the English language. What a lovely sound! Home: what does that make you think of? Sometimes my mind goes back to the first home I can remember, 1917 Hilton Avenue in Ashland, Kentucky. I think of the security of home. You sometimes wish you could go back. Recently we drove to Ashland. Everything has changed, the house isn't the same. They have redone it and I wouldn't have known it was the same place. I was so disappointed. I can never go back.

We all have to move on and, as for Abraham, he had an opportunity to go back (Heb. 10:11). Perhaps you say, 'I am tired of this place!' You could go back. But Abraham made his home in the Promised Land. He just decided to make it home. What kind of home? Living in a tent! What a lifestyle! What a legacy! We might ask, 'Abraham, is that the best you are going to do for Isaac, for your grandchild, Jacob? Can't you do better than that for them?' Do you know what it's like to wish that your children ought to have better than that which you can provide?

I suppose it used to break my father's heart when I would go up to him as a boy and say, 'Dad, do you know what Mickey got for Christmas? Do you know what John got for Christmas? Do you know what Dick gets to do next summer? Why can't I go?' I don't think this blessed my father. He would say, 'Son, I am sorry, but I work for wages, my salary is $8 a day. We do our best.'

I guess we were among the poorest people in our neighbourhood; you would call us working class or, at best, lower middle class. I had to go to church every time the door was open. Other kids didn't have to do that. 'Dad, is that the best you can do for me, it's not fair!' Those were the conditions I was brought up in. But I have no complaints today. There may be young people who read these lines; they may resent the way they have been brought up. Perhaps you resent having Christian parents? You resent that you didn't have other things, but one day you will see how good to you God was. I now try to thank God all the time that he has been so good to me, giving me the parents that I had, a home like I had. One day you too will be thankful. Do you think Isaac and Jacob resented that their grandfather had left Mesopotamia years before, felt that they could be living back there? For all they had was living in tents!

In the case of Moses, we are told his new conditions were pretty bad. He chose not to be the son of Pharaoh's daughter. He chose to be ill-treated, and regarded disgrace for the sake of Christ as of greater value than the treasures of Egypt (Heb. 11:24–5). How could one experience disgrace for Christ 1,300 years before he came? Jesus said that Abraham saw his day – Jesus' day – and was 'glad' (John 8:56). Likewise, Moses saw prophetically that what he was doing prepared the way for what was coming. Not that he saw things as clearly as we do, and yet his anointing led him to embrace a stigma that prefigured the very reproach of Jesus.

What had happened was this: the children of Israel had come to live in the land of Goshen in Egypt, and because of who they were, and because of Joseph – who was Prime Minister – they were living in the best conditions. But overnight there was a Pharaoh who didn't know Joseph; Joseph had died. The new Pharaoh turned against the people of Israel, and those were awful days. Talk about unhappy living conditions! 'They made their lives bitter with hard labour in brick and mortar and with all kinds of work in the fields; in all their hard labour the Egyptians used them ruthlessly' (Exod. 1:14). Moses left the palace of Pharaoh to be identified with this people.

Later he went to the Pharaoh and said, 'Let my people go!' (Exod. 5:1). The thanks he got was that Pharaoh said, 'You are no longer to supply the people with straw for making bricks; let them go and gather their own straw. But require them to make the same number of bricks as before; don't reduce the quota. They are lazy; that is why they are crying out, "Let us go and sacrifice to our God." Make the work harder for the men so that they keep working and pay no attention to lies' (Exod. 5:7–9).

The living conditions went from bad to worse and the people began to complain more than ever, angry that Moses had ever looked their way (Exod. 5:21). But they were finally delivered from Pharaoh's bondage. Where were they living then? In the wilderness, in the desert. They again turned against Moses and said, 'It was better in Egypt!' Who would have thought that? Sometimes you may complain about where you are living and your conditions, and God lets you jump out of the frying pan into the fire. You think, 'I'd love to be back where I was!' That's the way they were. But they complained so much that they made God angry. God went to Moses and said, 'I am fed up with the people, I am going to destroy them and start a new nation with you!' Moses said, 'Oh no! Don't do that!' Moses was free to leave at any time he wanted; he could have left them. For example, he could have gone to live with Jethro, his father-in-law, but he stayed right there. 'So he said he would destroy them – had not Moses, his chosen one, stood in the breach before him to keep his wrath from destroying them' (Ps. 106:23). Moses accepted unhappy living conditions and stayed right there. Can you do that? Can you accept that God has put you where you are for a reason? It's not what you want to call home, but Abraham and Moses made it home. Look at Abraham's company, his legacy: he lived in tents, as did Isaac and Jacob, who were heirs with him of the same promises. They all experienced the same thing, family together, who happened to be the people of God.

We are told that the ordinary people heard Jesus gladly. We are told that God's people, by and large, are not aristocracy; they are not high-powered – just ordinary people (1 Cor. 1:26). Ordinary people come from ordinary homes. Moses suffered disgrace with the people of God. How would you like to spend all your time with God's people? Moses' problem was further complicated by living so physically close to those he had to be involved with.

Are you having to live with Christians? Are you having to live with family, but you get on each other's nerves – perhaps you would like some space? It's one thing to have family to stay for a day or two. My Grandpa McCurley used to say, 'Company are like fish. After three days they begin to stink.' He also used to say to us, 'Glad to see you come, glad to see you go!' But what if you have to live with people like that all the time? There is a reason for this but there is hope in it all: Abraham was 'looking forward to the city with foundations, whose architect and builder is God' (Heb. 11:10).

> All these people were still living by faith when they died. They did not receive the things

promised; they only saw them and welcomed them from a distance. And they admitted that they were aliens and strangers on earth. People who say such things show that they are looking for a country of their own. If they had been thinking of the country they had left, they would have had opportunity to return. Instead, they were longing for a better country – a heavenly one. Therefore God is not ashamed to be called their God, for he has prepared a city for them (Heb. 11:13–16).

The reason Abraham could endure these conditions, we are told, is because they were temporary. It wouldn't be like that for ever. When we are in Florida, I see the beautiful homes by the sea and on the waterways, and it is hard to take in such beauty. But I think to myself, that's probably all the owners of such homes will ever have. Those who just want nicer houses, more comfort, a little more luxury. For some it is not enough just to have ordinary plumbing fixtures, they want them made of gold. Some try to create a mansion here on earth. Jesus said, 'In my Father's house there are many mansions' (John 14:1, AV). Paul said, 'But our citizenship is in heaven' (Phil. 3:20). Whatever your conditions may be, whether it be living in a wheelchair or in a prison; whether you are in hospital or some awful situation, it's not for ever. For some, though, that's all they will ever have!

I remember once saying to the missionary Jackie Pullinger, 'Where is your home?' She just pointed upward and said, 'I really do mean that. Sometimes I can hardly wait.'

Abraham may have been the first man in the Old Testament to have a glimpse of heaven. It shows what God does with his people who make home into home, wherever they are – because they know it is not for ever.

Could it be that God has sent that thorn in the flesh so that we would get our real joy not from the situation around us, but from the joy of the Lord (Neh. 8:10)? Let us not be like the people of Israel who thought that Messiah would mainly change their living conditions. Have you thought, if I get closer to God he will change my living conditions? Instead, what God is possibly wanting to say is, 'Get closer to me and enjoy my presence.' So that we can say, whatever the situation, whatever the circumstances, whatever the neighbours are like, I will rejoice! Who knows how real God will be to you, all because those unhappy living conditions drove you to seek his face – which is the reason he allowed it, to get your attention.

So this is the compensation – the joy of the Lord. Moses even had a pragmatic reason for doing what he did. If some journalist had gone up to Moses and said, 'Am I right in believing that you left a palace to live here, with these people?' Moses would have said, 'Yes.' 'But why? Why?' Moses would have said, 'That's the easiest decision I have ever had to make. I regard disgrace for the sake of Christ as of greater value than the treasures of Egypt because I am looking ahead to my reward.' Moses was actually motivated by reward. Jesus himself was looking forward to what it would be like after the suffering (Heb. 12:2), but he despised the shame.

God could change our situation here below and maybe he will. When? I answer: the moment his presence becomes more precious than the external circumstances that we thought were so important. The Authorised Version says that Moses had respect unto the 'recompense of reward'. Moses knew that God rewards those who are committed. So Paul could say, 'To keep me from becoming conceited because of these surpassingly great revelations, there was given me a thorn in my flesh, a messenger of Satan, to torment me' (2 Cor. 12:7). Do you perhaps have a problem with conceit? Do you want to show off your home? Show off your situation? Paul said, 'I pleaded with the Lord three times, take it away!' Maybe you have prayed, 'Oh God, let me have a better place to live! Move that neighbour! Move that person that I am having to live with, that I am so near, please remove them!' The Lord said to Paul, ' "My grace is sufficient for you, for my power is made perfect in weakness." Therefore I [Paul] will boast all the more gladly about my weaknesses, so that Christ's power may rest on me. That is why, for Christ's sake, I delight in weaknesses, in insults, in hardships, in persecutions, in difficulties. For when I am weak, then I am strong' (2 Cor. 12:9–10). David says, 'For the LORD God is a sun and shield; the LORD bestows favour and honour; no good thing does he withhold from those whose walk is blameless' (Ps. 84:11). So those unhappy living conditions, lack of space, difficult company, difficult neighbours, lack of comfort, will one day be seen as part of God's plan and will be treasured. I repeat, Israel's mistake was thinking that the purpose of Messiah was to create better living conditions. Could it be that you really have thought that if you could only get God's attention, he would change everything for you? What he has in mind is that we might know his presence. God will not let any of us get too attached to a situation here on earth.

I recall the story of the returning missionary who had spent forty years in Africa; he was going home to America. The big ship sailed into New York harbour, and as it was being moored the old missionary heard a band playing. He said to himself, 'Ah, they shouldn't have done that for me!' He could envisage his friends getting a band to welcome him home, but when he tried to get off the ship, they said, 'Stop right here, please!' It turned out that President Theodore Roosevelt was on the ship – he also was returning from Africa. He had been there for three weeks, big game hunting. The band of course was playing for the President of the United States. Roosevelt got off the ship first, was welcomed, and away he went. The old missionary was the last person to get off the ship. He walked down the gangplank and looked around, holding his suitcases. There was nobody there, nobody. He made his way to an old third-rate hotel in Manhattan and fell down on his knees. He said, 'Lord, why? The President of the United States goes to Africa for three weeks and a band is playing for him when he comes home, and I come home after forty years and there's nobody!' Then he heard God whisper to him, 'But you're not home yet!'

We must understand the message of Abraham, Isaac, Jacob and Moses: that this life is not all there is. The more we set our sight on that city that has foundations whose builder and maker is God, then the little bit of heaven that God will give us on the way to heaven will be the greatest compensation. 'For the kingdom of God is not a matter of eating and drinking, but of righteousness, peace and joy in the Holy Spirit' (Rom. 14:17).

7

A sexual misgiving

I deal now with a most sensitive subject – when one's thorn in the flesh may be a sexual misgiving. This is, perhaps, the most delicate chapter of this book. Victor Hugo said that fools rush in where angels fear to tread, and yet this area of sexual misgiving is undoubtedly very close to many, many people. A great number of Christians worry about sex and their own sexuality.

The word 'misgiving' means a feeling of doubt, slight fear or mistrust. So a sexual misgiving is a feeling of doubt, fear or lack of confidence about one's sexuality or lack of sexual identity; an area where you have a fear about your sexuality. It is when you are worried that something is wrong with you. You mistrust yourself. As a result, some people do not form good personal relationships. People like this are afraid to get married. Many are even afraid to get involved in a heterosexual relationship.

This brings me to some definitions. The word 'heterosexual' means having a desire for the opposite sex: a man desiring a woman, a woman desiring a man. 'Homosexual' is having a desire for the same sex. 'Asexual' is where there is no strong sexual feeling either way. I

117

will be writing a good bit about homosexuality. I could have made this explicit in the chapter title, but did not do so for three reasons.

First, there are sexual misgivings in heterosexual men and women, and possibly just as many problems. Heterosexual men have fears that range from doubts about masculinity and virility to an unease about intimacy with the opposite sex. Likewise, some women fear there is something wrong with them if they are not interested in sex. The second reason is therefore because we *all* have some fears, if we are honest, when it comes to sex or sexuality. We are afraid we won't live up to expectations, or that we will disappoint and be disappointed. These fears persist even after marriage. We think there must be something very wrong with us. The third reason is nobody is perfect. The James Bonds of this world exist only in people's fantasies or Hollywood films.

Why have I chosen to write on this matter under the general theme of 'thorn in the flesh'? The first reason I do so is because there are those who think – or hope – that this really was Paul's thorn in the flesh. In medieval times, the theory that Paul's thorn was carnal desire began to spread widely at a time when people were entering monasteries or convents to escape the dangers of sexual temptation. Yet many people found that they *still* had the problem of carnal desire in monasteries and convents in a way that they weren't prepared for. So they began to conjecture that this was Paul's problem as well: they supposed that Paul's special affliction was akin to what was a special difficulty in themselves.

This theory persists to the present day. There are those

who are gay who have even gone so far as to claim that this was Paul's problem. 'Now if I do what I do not want to do, it is no longer I who do it, but it is sin living in me that does it' (Rom. 7:20). Isn't it amazing how we want so much to superimpose our own hang-up or tendency on to a particular scripture?

What we *do* know is that Paul doesn't say what his thorn in the flesh is; while on earth, we will never know. May I repeat yet again, he uses a metaphor, a figure of speech, so that any of us can identify with it. I personally doubt that Paul himself was referring to sexual frustration, but I do not doubt that he used a metaphor by which those who do have such can feel accepted by God. I am sure there are Christians who do have a sexual misgiving, and why shouldn't they find strength and comfort from 2 Corinthians 12:7? That is why I write this chapter. I write this hoping that every single reader will not feel odd, second-class, unloved, pigeon-holed or categorised, but simply accepted. Not just by me, but by the Lord Jesus. I write this not only for those who are bothered by homosexual temptation, but also for those who are heterosexual yet who have all kinds of sexual misgivings.

I reached the conclusion that this is a subject I should deal with also because it puts a sexual misgiving into perspective. A thorn in the flesh is painful. That means, we wish it weren't there. If you are proud of your particular thorn in the flesh and are glad it's there for the wrong reason, so that you want to flaunt it, you've missed the whole point. For when we call it a thorn in the flesh it is in stark contrast to the attitudes being thrust upon us so often today. What once was regarded as something that should be kept in secret and to oneself is now brought out into the open, and some people want to give respectability in a manner that the Bible would not do. So if it is a thorn in the flesh, then you are going to wish you didn't have it rather than say, 'This is wonderful, why don't you have it as well!' People who advertise and boast of being gay or lesbian have missed the whole point. If you are a Christian, please don't ever align yourself with those who do that. It is private and personal, so if it is your thorn, it means you are not going to be telling the world.

I also want to stress that having such a proclivity doesn't mean you should feel second-class. One's sexual proclivity has nothing to do with whether one is a Christian, or even a spiritual person. The word 'proclivity' is one thing, 'practice' is another. Proclivity is just a word that means tendency. So you can have a tendency towards homosexuality and not give in – any robustly heterosexual man or woman is resisting temptation all the time.

What is it like to have a sexual misgiving? It is a continual fear or doubt concerning one's sexuality – whether homosexual, heterosexual or asexual. There are those, for example, who fear they are gay when they are not. This has long been a problem with people who are genuinely afraid that they are gay, possibly because of an experience that goes right back to childhood. They may have been abused by a friend of the same age, and then got involved; all their lives they think that they must be gay. Sadly, many in the gay world would applaud and say, 'Yes! Be proud of it!' But you're not proud of it, you are afraid that you are that way when you are not.

There are those who are gay and admit to themselves that they are, and don't sweep it under the carpet. But they fear that they are not loved by the Lord, that there must be something spiritually wrong with them. They fear that there's no chance they could ever be godly and be a true servant of Jesus Christ.

There are also people who are heterosexual and happily married, but still doubt their sexuality. Some have a sexual misgiving because they are not happy with their husband or wife and they blame themselves. They feel guilty that they don't enjoy or desire sexual intimacy. Some have an unhappy marriage (a subject covered in the next chapter) because of lack of sexual fulfilment. That in itself could be one's thorn in the flesh.

Some Christians feel guilty, whether married or single, because they aren't particularly interested in sex at all. They really aren't bothered. They don't have any great sexual desire, never have had. Or maybe they once did but don't now, and that worries them. They feel something is wrong with them and they hide this fear deep inside and almost never talk about it.

On the other hand, there are those who feel an almost overpowering desire for sexual fulfilment; they feel they are 'over-sexed'. They fear they are not normal. Some live in perpetual condemnation that they aren't really right with God or they wouldn't feel this way. There are people who have never found – and possibly never will find – a partner, and who have to cope with continual frustration. My heart goes out to such people. But Jesus understood: 'For we do not have a high priest who is unable to sympathise with our weaknesses, but we have one who has been tempted in every way, just as we are – yet was without sin' (Heb. 4:15). This included sexual temptation as well.

The list is endless. I think it is largely true that what worries many Christians has nothing to do with sin at all but pseudo-guilt (false guilt) because of the temptation or awareness of it. You let it stand between you and God. There are those who are, on the one hand, frigid or impotent; on the other hand, there are those who feel 'over-sexed'. Both categories think they are not right with God. There are those who only get their fulfilment from flirting because they fear intimacy. I have given here just a few examples – the list, as I said, is endless.

Why are people like this? Why does one have this fear of sex, or of one's own sexuality? What is the cause of a sexual misgiving? Generally speaking, all behaviour is in some sense caused. There is a big debate among psychologists and geneticists as to whether we are motivated by heredity or environment. A while ago there was a general consensus that we are predominantly governed by the effects upon us of environment – family, friends, education, culture and other influences. But the pendulum has begun to swing the other way, with a growing belief that heredity may have a stronger influence after all. For one thing, twins who have been separated at birth, but rediscovered each other many years later, have been found to be astonishingly similar despite totally different living conditions. Whatever the reality, Dr Clyde Narramore of the Narramore Christian Foundation in California says: 'Every person is worth understanding.' If you only knew what was in the background of a particular person, you would lower your voice. This should help us not to judge others, but instead help us to understand them.

There is one who understands – Jesus: 'Because he himself suffered when he was tempted, he is able to help those who are being tempted' (Heb. 2:18). We do indeed have a great high priest who is able to sympathise with our weaknesses (Heb. 4:15). This sympathy is something you may not find in another person, for they may not understand. Sometimes, however, it may be best that you don't find sympathy. I say this for this reason. If a person has a sexual weakness and you go to another person because you think they too may have the same sexual weakness, you are probably not going to get help. You are going to make the situation ten times, a hundred times, worse: 'The heart is deceitful above all things and beyond cure. Who can understand it?' (Jer. 17:9). We think we are going to help or get help, but often the temptation to sexual sin is only heightened and we are worse off than ever. Often the desire to help is a camouflage, sometimes a conscious one, to get closer to a person for the wrong reasons. The worst thing you can do if you have a particular sexual weakness is to think that you can go to another person because he or she has it too. This, then, is the exception to the rule, for usually it is wonderful to find one other person who knows what we are going through. But when it comes to sex, and the other person has the same problem, don't do it!

Jesus understands; he utterly sympathises. If this is your

thorn in the flesh, the reason you've got it is to develop intimacy with Jesus who sympathises and understands. If you can get your identity from knowing you are approved by him, you are making considerable progress.

There is a reason we are like we are – for example, unsatisfactory relationships with parents. There are two extremes. One extreme is a parent – a mother or father – who never hugs their children. Do you realise just how damaging that is to a child? I'm telling any parent, if this is you, then you are hurting your child. The Prince of Wales is quoted as saying that he cannot remember being hugged after he was eight years old. I am so glad that my parents hugged me. My mother hugged me, my father hugged me. From the first day I can remember, my parents hugged me and, after I grew up, they kept hugging me; it never stopped. Not hugging is one extreme.

The other extreme is abuse. That is where a child has been abused by a parent, a relative or an older person. Such a trauma, though not always noticeable at the time (by the abused or even others nearby), has a time-bomb effect which later on causes people to doubt themselves and their sexuality. They don't know what is wrong with them. They suppose that *they* must have done something to make their father, their mother, their uncle want to do that. 'There must be something wrong with me,' they say.

So there is a reason for the way we are, and it often goes back to our relationship with parents or authority figures. There is no substitute for a good relationship that begins in the home.

There is yet another reason. Sex is very powerful if only because of the hype from Hollywood, television and the way people talk about it. It can therefore be very frightening – it can lead to a fear of sex, especially if one has a low self-esteem.

I have to say, sadly, though I wish it weren't true, that in some cases no amount of counselling, psychotherapy or psychoanalysis seems to compensate for a deprived childhood. So if you had a good, secure parental back-ground, thank God! Pray for the growing generation around you who don't have what you had. Someone said, 'They say childhood is the best time of your life. I say childhood is what you spend the rest of your life trying to recover from.' How dare we, then, judge another when they have got their problems. We are without excuse. God has been good to us. You say, 'I haven't got that problem!' Yes, you were blessed, but has it turned you into a self-righteous, judgmental person? You too may get judged; it's only a matter of time, one way or another. Jesus said, 'Do not judge, or you too will be judged' (Matt. 7:1).

But I want also to offer comfort to any parent reading this who has children who have sexual misgivings, and you blame yourself. No parent is perfect. We are all products of imperfect parents to some degree. This is partly what is meant by 'he punishes the children and their children for the sin of the fathers to the third and fourth generation' (Exod. 34:7). It is a chain reaction. One hopes that when it gets to us we will stop it – and be the perfect parent. Oh, I wish it were true!

To go into it in a little more detail, what exactly are some possible causes for sexual misgivings, especially homosexuality? The domineering mother or the absentee father has long been regarded as a cause. Some believe (I think there is some truth to this) that homosexuality is to be explained by the lack of a good relationship with the parent of the same sex. In this case, homosexual tendencies show the need to make good that relationship. So if a mother and a daughter do not have a good relationship, it is possible that that daughter will want to make good that relationship by seeking intimate female companions. This is not always the case, but is sometimes regarded as a cause. The same is true with father and son, where the son does not have a good relationship with his father and he looks for fulfilment with men and so make good the relationship. What I do know is that a large number of people who are gay will admit to a lack of love from their parents. This shows the importance of getting it right in the home; the family unit is so important. There are those who rightly stress the importance of a solid family: mother and father who love their children and no separation and no divorce. The ideal, of course, is where there is love and security. There is no substitute for this. It won't do merely to make political statements. What is needed is revival, an awakening, where people are converted and then are taught the ideals. This is the need of the hour and God knows we need it soon.

Some years ago I gave a series of sermons on this and they became a book: *Is God for the Homosexual?* It is now out of print; it was anything but a best-seller. Many thought it would be a best-seller because I didn't condemn homosexuality, but when some people kept reading and saw that the Bible *does* condemn the practice, they didn't like the book. But I remember during that series we had a person who professed faith in Christ and he still keeps in touch with me; I dedicated that book to him. His father hated him. He told me (he would break down and weep) the things that his father would say to him. It makes one feel so sympathetic.

Take child abuse where the child, as he or she gets older, blames himself or herself, and doesn't feel normal. Consider also those who are sent to boarding schools, often a breeding ground for homosexuality. If the age of consent is lowered, all it will do is validate this.

Others (not just homosexuals, but heterosexuals too) are often never the same after rape, or being in prison. Or some, even after they get married, feel unloved – and therefore doubt their own sex appeal and their sexual identity.

Yet one would also have to add that a cause of a sexual misgiving is sometimes due to the lack of good teaching. Sex is best taught in the home, and when sex education validates alternative lifestyles it is damaging.

In a word: all behaviour, including sexual misgivings, in a sense has a cause. It almost always goes back to the past, usually stemming from childhood.

But God knows that. Joni Eareckson Tada's book *When God Weeps* shows how God weeps with us. I'm sure that concept took a lot of courage for her to embrace, for Joni is reformed in her theology, and has got one of the best theological minds I have come across. Most reformed people will not accept the idea that God weeps. Maybe Jesus, but not the Father. It goes back to the idea that God cannot feel pain, that he is impassive.

That idea is not in the Bible, but is part of what has been inherited from Greek philosophy. Joni shows how God weeps, and I am sure that God feels what you may have felt as you were growing up and these things were happening.

Why does God permit it? You tell me. There's no end to the speculation about why God allows evil. God will one day explain that, but he has sent his Son who was the victim of the greatest evil of all. Look at the way he was crucified, look at the way he had no trial. And even this was God's plan, if only to let you know that he knows what you feel. He has given us a Saviour who was tempted at all points like we are. Some of us, though, after we get through a situation, or have a victory, quickly forget – and soon start pointing the finger. 'Oh well, I got a victory over this! Oh, I don't have that problem any more!' But we may have another kind – ten times worse. Jesus, however, never forgot what it was like.

There is a big difference between misgiving and sin. That you aren't perfect sexually doesn't mean that you are not Christian, that you are not well adjusted; nor does it mean you are not spiritual. My grandmother used to say that the best way to live a long time is to get something wrong with you and take care of it! I think there is a lot of truth to that. Well, the thorn in the flesh can be like that, for this reason: it will humble you. It should keep you from being self-righteous. It should keep you from being conceited. It should drive you to God every day, and the result will be an intimacy with the Father that you wouldn't have had. In other words, had you not had that particular problem it might not have driven you to God.

When you get to heaven, do not be surprised that that which you felt so awful about – whether it was your heterosexual drive or homosexual tendency, or no sexual feelings at all – was used by God for your good. It worries you now, but when you get to heaven you will see that God was being gracious to you, because that was the best way to get your attention – not to mention keep you from being self-righteous.

Another important clarification that we have already touched upon is the difference between the proclivity and the practice. Being gay or lesbian by tendency is not the same thing as carrying this out. Proclivity is not sinning, the practice is. It wouldn't surprise me if when we get to heaven, it turns out that there have been many, many great men and women of God who had this temptation secretly. Frederick W. Faber, the hymn writer, was a non-practising homosexual. There is a famous hymn that he wrote and I can hardly say the words without them bringing tears to my eyes, knowing that this was his problem:

> There's a wideness in God's mercy
> Like the wideness of the sea;
> There's a kindness in his justice
> That is more than liberty.

There is a difference here between temptation and sin. It is not a sin to be tempted. Jesus was tempted; Jesus didn't sin. If you are tempted, do not condemn yourself. Even Jesus was tempted and he wasn't born with sin; he didn't even have original sin. He was born of a virgin, was sinless, and yet he was tempted like we are. We who are a part of a fallen race have this to fight. Our Lord Jesus knows what it was like for him when he was without sin. He truly sympathises.

Another clarification is this: pseudo-guilt may come from temptation; real guilt by giving in. But I must say, if you are feeling guilty because you are tempted, then you 'ain't seen nothing yet!' If you give in, then you have to live with what you did. It is the devil who will make you feel guilty because you have got a particular weakness, even if you are asexual, which might make you feel odd, or strange. In this case, you may want to try to prove you are 'sexy'. There are those who actually let themselves get involved because they want to make a statement. They want to prove that they are not odd. The devil will lead you to do that, and then you are really going to have guilt. True guilt. Not pseudo-guilt, which is false guilt. Being tempted sometimes leads to pseudo-guilt. Real guilt is when you give in.

There is a difference between secret, personal embarrassment and public flaunting. If your temptation happens to be in a homosexual direction, I have to say, lovingly and firmly, that the Bible calls it unnatural. You will say, 'But it is natural to me', and I know what you mean by that. When you feel something you think, 'Well, it's natural.' But the fact that it *feels* natural doesn't mean what God means by that. For God created Adam and Eve male and female: 'So God created man in his own image, in the image of God he created him; male and female he created them' (Gen. 1:27). For that reason, because of the creation ordinance, what is natural is male and female. Heterosexual attraction for each other is the way God made us. This is why in Romans Paul uses very descriptive language – so descriptive that for years there were churches who wouldn't read it publicly: 'Because of this, God gave them over to shameful lusts. Even their women exchanged natural relations for unnatural ones' (Rom. 1:26). Leviticus 18:22 also made it absolutely clear, 'Do not lie with a man as one lies with a woman; that is detestable.' The New Testament in the New International Version calls it 'perversion' (Rom. 1:27). If you are a Christian, you will keep quiet about this matter. When this is flaunted today and people call themselves 'Christian gays' – proud of it – it is quite wrong. The phrase today is 'coming out', as if this were a heroic thing to do. It is not. If you are a Christian and you see it as a thorn in the flesh, you will likewise see that flaunting this is not honouring to the name of Christ and the Church. It is between you and God. God has allowed it to happen for your good.

Is there a cure for a sexual misgiving? Using the word 'cure' could be a little bit misleading, but I will explain why I use this word since, if this is your thorn in the flesh, it is probably a life sentence. Most sexual misgivings do not go away – either by conversion, deep consecration or good counselling. There are exceptions of course, and I thank God for the exceptions, but to hold up those exceptions to others as the norm would almost certainly add needless guilt to many people. I have known of sexual transformations of people as a result of conversion. Conversion certainly changes the lifestyle of the adulterer, and sometimes a homosexual person adopts a heterosexual lifestyle. Counselling can also help, but only if the person wants help.

What, then, is the cure if the misgiving does not go away? (1) Know that God accepts you and Jesus accepts you. (2) Resist temptation. One cure for guilt is not sinning. (3) Do not justify your weakness as though it is right. Accept it as a personal and private matter. Do not advertise it and, if you must tell someone, share it with somebody who doesn't have the same problem. If your worry is that you are asexual, that you have got little or no sex drive at all, keep quiet about that as well – and thank God that you've got perhaps the least painful of the thorns in the flesh. If your problem is being married and there's lack of sexual fulfilment, sympathise with your wife or husband. It's difficult for you, but it is difficult for him or for her as well:

> The husband should fulfil his marital duty to his wife, and likewise the wife to her husband. The wife's body does not belong to her alone but also to her husband. In the same way, the husband's body does not belong to him alone but also to his wife. Do not deprive each other except by mutual consent and for a time, so that you may devote yourselves to prayer. Then come together again so that Satan will not tempt you because of your lack of self-control (1 Cor. 7:3–5).

That is godly wisdom. Moreover, 'Wives, submit to your husbands as to the Lord' (Eph 5:22). But remember Ephesians 5:25: 'Husbands, love your wives, just as Christ loved the church and gave himself up for her . . .' First, it says, wives submit to your husbands, then husbands love your wives as Christ loved the Church and gave himself for it. So husbands should love their wives as their own bodies.

If you are unmarried, know that sexual intercourse outside marriage is sin. You will never have peace by giving in; the only cure is abstinence. If you are single you may feel you must remain that way because of sexual misgivings. This is so common. You may be sexually frustrated. You may fear that this frustration is rooted in either fear of your sexuality or being 'over-sexed'. God understands your feelings better than you do, and if he wants you to be married he will bring that person into your life who will love you as you are. You may also feel a sexual misgiving because you fear you have no sex appeal. This may be even more common than the previous example. 'Beauty is only skin deep', we used to hear, and I believe this is true. Sex appeal is much the same. When you get to know another person, sex appeal often surfaces in a surprising way. When you sense that the other person is attracted to you, a hidden sexual power inside will emerge – for the right person. Never forget: sex is a physical thing as well as a psychological one. It is the way God made us. A hidden sex appeal – until the right person comes along – may turn out to be what saved you from tragedy and, consequently, was the best thing that could have happened for you.

What if you have sinned? I have not written this chapter to make anyone feel odd, ashamed or guilty. But if you have sinned, 'If we confess our sins, he is faithful and just and will forgive us our sins and purify us from all unrighteousness' (1 John 1:9). Confess your sin and stop it! Never again.

I have reason to believe this is relevant for many Christians. Remember that it is not a thorn unless it hurts, but if you sin by running from the pain, you will be in more pain down the road. That thorn is God's means of getting your attention to keep you humble and bring you into intimacy with the Father.

8

An unhappy marriage

I doubt that an unhappy marriage was Paul's thorn and yet it cannot be ruled out. Clement of Rome in AD 95 said that Paul was married and that his wife did not travel with him on his missionary journeys. Although it is vague, and you can't prove it either way, Paul did say, 'Don't we have the right to take a believing wife along with us, as do the other apostles and the Lord's brothers and Cephas?' (1 Cor. 9:5). We all have a thorn in the flesh; God knows our frame, he remembers that we are dust (Ps. 103:14). He knows what it takes to get our attention, and the way in which he does this is through pain. It works. It hurts. We say, 'Yes Lord!' as a result.

There is no such thing as a perfect marriage, yet many are disillusioned only because they had unrealistic expectations in the first place. Do you know, for example, what it is like to look forward to a holiday for months and months? You fantasise, play music that is recognisably from that part of the world where you are going. You look forward to it so much. You plan to do things that you have read about in the guidebooks and other literature about the place. You have heard about the restaurants and the food. You are going to do this and that. And then finally, when the holiday comes, everything goes wrong. It's not the place that you envisaged. Furthermore, it rains. Things that were supposed to happen, don't. You are so disappointed. It was more fun looking forward to the holiday than the actual thing.

Well, that can be true in marriage. The looking-forward part is sometimes, sadly, more fun and exciting than the actual event. It will be interesting to learn when we get to heaven just how many sovereign vessels – God's special people, men and women – had had an unhappy marriage. John Wesley and George Whitefield were not happily married men. Neither really knew the joy of marital bliss. They were married, but it was a nightmare for each of them. Wesley's wife would come to hear her husband preach, and then cackle during the service. Can you imagine that?

Read in the Old Testament about Abigail; she was married to Nabal. Yet because of her bad marriage, God used her in the life of David. We wouldn't even know about Abigail if it weren't for her unhappy marriage. She was a sovereign vessel (1 Sam. 25). Madame Guyon, the seventeenth-century French mystic whose biography is worth reading, was God's gift to the world. Yet we wouldn't know about her if she hadn't had a miserable marriage.

There are also heartbreaking accounts of how some of God's best didn't marry the one they were in love with, and settled for someone else. They spent the rest of their lives wondering what it would have been like to have married the one they loved. But God can use this sort of thing. In my opinion, John Wesley, because of his cruel wife, was more refined as a man. It probably had a lot to do with his teaching on perfect love.

An unhappy marriage hardly needs defining. We are talking about when you are stuck with spending the rest of your life with someone with whom you are not happy. It is a thorn in the flesh, it is painful. Paul said he prayed three times for his particular situation to be resolved; perhaps *you* have prayed thirty-three times, or even three thousand and thirty-three times, for your situation to improve. You grew up and fantasised about that perfect wife, that perfect husband. In your dreams you saw only bliss. Enjoying companionship, affection, love, sharing, growing old together gracefully with the father or mother of your children. But no, it has been anything but bliss. You have watched others separate and you have envied them. They get divorced and you think, 'I wish that could happen to me', but you've stuck it out. You are not happy.

Can this actually describe a Christian? Yes. Does God truly want this in a Christian marriage? No. But when there is a breakdown, perhaps the best way to analyse it, at least for one if not both of the spouses, is to see this as your thorn in the flesh. God has allowed it. Satan exploits it; God let it happen. It is permitted by God, and yet paradoxically it is also a messenger of Satan to torment. So the devil exploits the situation. The devil knows every weakness that you've got. Your husband, your wife, knows every weakness you have. And the devil will get one person to focus upon the other's weakness. The devil will get you to remember every bad thing your husband, your wife, has done. In the crunch, when the crisis comes, you pull out that record and you begin to read every wrong.

What causes a breakdown in marriage? It often begins with a sad discovery. You are living with a person who is not what he or she appeared to be during the time of courtship. You wake up one day and say, 'This is a different person!' In courtship, one is on his or her best behaviour. You try to impress, you dress to impress, you look good, you try to please in every way, you don't want the thing to be called off. Once the marriage is finalised, it's locked in; you think, 'I can relax now.' The other person, though, says, 'You are not the person I married.' The sad discovery then is that there is not much real love here. You may discover that this person doesn't really love you. He or she married you for the wrong reason. You may discover you don't really love him, you don't really love her. What a sad discovery!

Marriage breakdown may come from a sudden disclosure, even after years of marriage, or financial problems you weren't prepared for, or relatives who mean more to your spouse than to you. Physical problems may emerge, although you thought that wouldn't happen in your case. You may well remember the marriage vow, 'For better for worse, for richer for poorer, in sickness and in health', and perhaps you said, 'Ah, but we're not going to have physical problems, we're not going to have financial problems.' You meant those vows, but you didn't think you would have to fall back on them.

There may be a sudden disclosure of sexual incompatibility. It turns out that your husband, or your wife, doesn't really enjoy, or want, sex. Or maybe you don't really want sex. You see it as your thorn; she or he sees it as their thorn.

Another kind of marriage breakdown is what I call the silent development, when a lack of deep respect almost imperceptibly sets in. For any marriage to survive there must be a foundation of admiration and respect. When respect has gone, the marriage is on the rocks. A lack of communication suddenly becomes the focus of the thorn. The husband or the wife withdraws. She says, 'Talk to me!' and he is irritable. He may plead, 'Couldn't I share this with you?' and she withdraws. The suggestion from one partner that they ought to talk just produces annoyance in the other, who would prefer to watch television or do something else.

The silent development is also evident when a job comes before the family; this person lives for his or her job or career and the family takes a back seat. This is my own failure – or, rather, one of them. I can recall those days (I would give anything in the world to turn the clock back and to have put my family first) when my church meant more to me than my family. I justified it, claiming, 'God put me here, I am called to preach.' I thought that I was putting God first. I doubt it. I say again that if I could re-live the last twenty-two years and spend more time with my family and less in preparing sermons, I would preach just as well, maybe even better.

Another silent development is when lack of similar interests widens and you marvel that you were ever attracted to the other person in the first place; you find you've got so little in common after all.

Marriage breakdown may be traced to spiritual defects. This is where one or both partners lose interest in spiritual things. Sometimes it is the opposite – that is, one becomes more interested in spiritual things and leaves the other behind – and the one 'ahead' just longs for one's spouse to enjoy God at a deeper level. And if it's not there, it hurts – and then what sometimes happens is that one begins to keep a record of wrongs. Why would someone do this? Perhaps because by making the other person look bad you can cover up any defect you have. We keep records to refer to them. You may say, 'I won't forget that!' and you are true to your word. At the right moment you pull out the record, as I said, and you start to read. You recall every bad incident. You are like the devil when you do that, for the devil is the accuser (Rev. 12:11). Whenever you point the finger, you are not being Jesus, you are being the devil.

Part of the fall-out of marriage breakdown is trying to figure out what has happened and what has been going on. You are overwhelmed with confusion. 'How could this happen to me?' 'How could I let myself marry this person?' 'Why did God permit me to marry this monster or this insensitive human being?' Nothing adds up. Nothing makes sense. 'I prayed for the right person and I fell in love, or thought I did, and now it's too late.'

The outlook becomes bleak, so unpromising, like a long, cold, bleak winter that lies ahead. You feel locked into a prison sentence and it's a life sentence. Marriage, according to the Bible, is for life: 'For this reason a man will leave his father and mother and be united to his wife, and they will become one flesh' (Gen. 2:24). My father used to warn me as I grew up, and would say, 'Marriage is for life!' It is, and that's why you want to get it right. If you can ever manage to get things right once in your life, you want it to be when you get married. Divorce was never God's idea. God says through Malachi, 'I hate divorce' (Mal. 3:16). After all, Christ and his Church never got divorced.

If I have described you, what do you do now? Where do you go from here? My answer is this: this is your free ticket for intimacy with God. If you let this thorn be the means of bringing you to intimacy with God, to a place where you get to know him, you will eventually thank God for it all. Up to now you have said, 'Oh, I know the Lord. Jesus is my Saviour and I pray to him.' But then you realise after many years, you haven't really got to know God. When you do get to know God, you realise, 'Oh, I didn't really know him before.' It is when you truly experience how real he is: 'However, as it is written: "No eye has seen, no ear has heard, no mind has conceived what God has prepared for those who love him" ' (1 Cor. 2:9). All because of an unhappy marriage, it drove you to God. It is also what will lead you to a reward at the judgment seat of Christ. You may say, 'I don't worry about that!' But when it comes, it will mean everything. It may be that you have been smug – '*I'm* very well, thank you.' But then suddenly God comes into your life, so powerfully that you realise what really matters: that one day you will have a reward that you wouldn't have had otherwise. God had to get your attention. We all need a thorn. Is an unhappy marriage your thorn?

This bleakness, sadly, often becomes bitterness. The reality begins to set in. 'I am stuck! Things are not going to get better.' Then there is real bitterness. You say, 'Life is passing me by! I wanted companionship; I am not getting it. I wanted to be admired; I am not admired, I am not respected. I wanted to be loved; I don't feel loved. I wanted sexual fulfilment; I'm not getting that!'

The Holy Spirit is a person, a very sensitive person. He can be grieved (Eph. 4:30), he can be quenched (1 Thess. 5:19). The primary way we grieve the Spirit is by bitterness: 'Get rid of all bitterness, rage and anger, brawling and slander, along with every form of malice. Be kind and compassionate to one another, forgiving each other, just as in Christ God forgave you' (Eph. 4:31–2). If this bitterness is not dealt with, Satan erects a stronghold and this can seem insurmountable. And yet this stronghold can be dismantled when we are devoid of bitterness and learn to forgive. Totally. For the stronghold is in the mind. If we rid ourselves of bitterness, Satan loses his grip: 'The weapons we fight with are not the weapons of the world. On the contrary, they have divine power to demolish strongholds. We demolish arguments and every pretension that sets itself up against the knowledge of God, and we take captive every thought to make it obedient to Christ' (2 Cor. 10:4–5).

Sometimes a blueprint for a bad marriage was there from the start – it was there from the beginning but you hadn't noticed it. Now to be fair, you can't always tell in advance. Even the best kind of pre-marriage counselling and preparation doesn't necessarily prepare you for everything. But there are certain things that ought to be warning signs. Why do I write like this? For one thing, it is to let people know that they are not alone. God permitted your problem for a purpose, so there is no need to panic. I write also for any single person who feels disillusioned that maybe they are not going to get married. There is something worse than being single, and that is to be married – but *unhappily*. I write also to let any unmarried person who hopes to get married know what pitfalls there are and how you might have a blue-print for a successful marriage. What is the blueprint that forecasts in advance why a marriage will be unhappy? Well, there are several things.

First, you may have married too soon. You couldn't wait. You wouldn't listen.

Second, as I said at the beginning of this chapter, you could have had unrealistic expectations. One of the best books on marriage I have read puts forward the thesis that the reason marriages go wrong is because there is often an unconscious desire on the part of the man to find in his wife the love he really didn't have from his mother. There is, equally, the unconscious desire on the part of the woman, when she marries this man, to get the love she didn't have from her father. Therefore, whatever deprivation there was as you grew up – even if it was unconscious – the reason you chose who you did was because you thought this person was going to make up for that deprivation you had when you were a child. But of course it never works out that way, and you get angry and accuse your spouse for not meeting a need when in fact you chose that person because you were thinking of yourself! So if you are wanting the father you never had, don't blame your husband; he can't be everything. If you are wanting the mother you never had, realise that your wife can't be everything. You married a wife, not a mother.

Third, you may have married for appearance's sake. I refer not merely to good looks. You married, perhaps, to please your parents. The whole time you were with this man or young lady, you thought, 'Dad will like this one!' So you were thinking the whole time, 'What will my parents think?' You never really took seriously the question, 'What do *I* feel?' You married for appearance's sake. She's beautiful, he's handsome. He's got such a good background, this will go down really well with my parents. Or friends. He's got a good job.

Fourth, you may have married in panic. You thought you would never get married if you didn't grab this opportunity with both hands, and so you jumped out of the frying pan into the fire.

Fifth, some marry for sex only. The first thing on some people's minds is the last thing that will hold a marriage together. Martin Luther said, 'God uses sex to drive a person to marriage.' But *eros* love, the physical attraction that God gave us and made us with, will not by itself keep one's marriage going. *Agape* love has got to parallel *eros* love or the marriage will eventually end up on the rocks. One famous film star is on husband number seven – she is still looking for that perfect man to keep her happy and satisfied. *Agape* love (which is described in 1 Corinthians 13) has got to come in or the marriage will break down.

Some get married because they were jilted, and then

marry on the rebound. This happens all too often. In this case, you not only live the rest of your life with the one you didn't want, but you married too soon because you were embarrassed, hurt or angry; you wanted to make a statement.

Is there any way that an unhappy marriage may turn into a blessing? Have you said to yourself, 'Is this all there is?' It is like going to that place on holiday when you say, 'Is this it? I've looked forward to *this*?' So with marriage. You say, 'Am I locked into a prison sentence?' Yet if you put Jesus Christ first, this nightmare of a marriage can be the greatest source of blessing.

I will say it again: it should drive one to intimacy with God. God is jealous; we were bought with a price – the price of the blood of his Son. God likes to spend time with us, he likes our company, but many of us have been too busy. We have justified being too busy and said, 'God understands.' The truth is, some didn't care that much about God; but God cared about them and, in order to get their attention, he sent this thorn in the flesh because he wants all of us to get to know him. The remedy may or may not revive your marriage, but it will revive you!

Your marriage may have a wonderful breakthrough. The grass is not greener on the other side of the fence; you may be the one to turn your marriage around. Don't wait for him, or her. Begin with yourself. I have found the old axiom to be true: when I change, my wife changes. When she changes, I change.

A the end of the day, it takes two. It's like a seesaw and both must work at it constantly. You may say that you are trying to work at it, but have found that you alone can't make it happen. But you may be surprised to learn what could develop further down the line if you decide to get it truly right in yourself. The recipe for this breakthrough is that you find inner peace, that you become vulnerable. You begin with yourself. Stop pointing the finger.

So don't try to change your partner – you change instead. You may say, 'Well, this isn't right!' But you are the one who is going to get the blessing! You change! Remember your biblical duty before the Lord.

Let us suppose you are the wife: 'Wives, submit to your husbands as to the Lord. For the husband is the head of the wife as Christ is the head of the church, his body, of which he is the Saviour. Now as the church submits to Christ, so also wives should submit to their husbands in everything' (Eph 5:22–4).

So if you are the wife, the Bible says, submit to your husband. You say, 'I can't!' But Paul goes on to talk about those who are slaves. 'Slaves, obey your earthly masters with respect and fear, and with sincerity of heart, just as you would obey Christ' (Eph. 6:5). Which would you prefer? Being a slave, having to obey one who isn't very nice to you, or being married and submitting to your husband? You may say, 'One would be as bad as the other!' That may well be true, but Paul said in Colossians 3.22: 'Slaves, obey your earthly masters in everything; and do it, not only when their eye is on you and to win their favour, but with sincerity of heart and reverence for the Lord.' So a slave is told to do this, and you may feel that's the way you are treated. I am not justifying this

146

situation and I'm not saying it's good. But if you do it for Jesus, and even say, 'Lord, I hate this but I want to please you', you may be surprised at the difference it could make in turning your marriage around.

But I have not finished. Paul says:

> Husbands, love your wives, just as Christ loved the church and gave himself up for her to make her holy, cleansing her by the washing with water through the word, and to present her to himself as a radiant church, without stain or wrinkle or any other blemish, but holy and blameless. In this same way, husbands ought to love their wives as their own bodies. He who loves his wife loves himself. After all, no-one ever hated his own body, but he feeds and cares for it, just as Christ does the church – for we are members of his body. 'For this reason a man will leave his father and mother and be united to his wife, and the two will become one flesh.' This is a profound mystery – but I am talking about Christ and the church. However, each one of you also must love his wife as he loves himself, and the wife must respect her husband (Eph. 5:25–33).

A wife must submit to a husband who is not very nice, and a husband must love his wife even if she, at the moment, may not seem lovable. This is the pattern. Husbands, love your wives. You never thought when you were engaged that you would need to be told that! 'Don't tell me how to love my wife, I'm crazy about her!'

you may say. But remember, a few months on, you may look across the breakfast table and think, 'What *have* I done?'

Can you see why Paul said, 'Love your wives'? That means you must respect her, build her up, care for her. This is the challenge to see whether you are a real man. Do you think you are a man merely because you can attract women? Do you think you are a man because of how strong you are? Because you are good-looking? Do you want to be a real man? Then love your wife! That is what builds character. Love her! 'When I became a man, I put childish ways behind me' (1 Cor. 13:11).

The recipe for the breakthrough, then, is don't try to change your partner; *you* change. The more I change, the more my wife Louise changes, and the more she changes, the more I change. It will not do for you to say to your husband, 'You don't love me and that's why I am not submitting to you!' Or for him to say, 'When you start submitting to me, I will love you! You're not submitting!' My guess is that a lot of wives wouldn't mind submitting to somebody they felt loved by.

Don't wait for the other person to get it right. Love your partner, no matter what! You might not win them round in one day, but somewhere down the line they may come to you and say, 'You were great! I was horrible!'

No marriage is perfect. I say it again, the grass is not greener on the other side of the fence. Most marriages can be saved, and you can fall in love all over again. Love Jesus Christ more than you love each other, and that way

you are going to love each other more than you otherwise ever would have. Don't wait for the other person to
get it right; and you may one day realise that that thorn is
part of a rose, beautiful and fragrant.

9

A chronic illness

There are many ways God can get our attention, and one of them is through chronic illness. Many Christians can identify with this. Some good people are ill almost continuously.

Some scholars also think this was actually Paul's thorn in the flesh, because he refers to the fact that at one time Galatian Christians would have plucked out their eyes for him (Gal. 4:15). He said he came to them because of an illness (Gal. 4:13). Thus his referring to his illness generally, and to his eyes in particular, has led to the belief that Paul had a chronic eye disease. This is a little bit speculative, but there is more evidence for this than perhaps on many other opinions of Paul's thorn. What we do know is that he certainly had a chronic illness; what we don't know is whether this was what he meant by his own thorn in the flesh. It could have been something other than that.

The truth is, many Christians have more than one thorn in the flesh, but often there is one in particular that preoccupies us. Again we must stress that Paul is using a figure of speech – a metaphor that we can all identify with it.

But I do know this – illness, even if it is temporary, is a thorn. It hurts. But if you have a chronic illness, then this is almost certainly going to be your thorn in the flesh. You must never forget that God has allowed this. You may say, 'I've prayed to be healed and he hasn't healed me.' That may also be a pretty strong hint that God doesn't want to heal you – yet. He is able to heal. We pray for healing at our church. We have had some unusual testimonies of healing in recent times – and if I said 'extraordinary' healings, that would not be far from the truth. We have heard wonderful testimonies. I hope the day will come when God will trust us with a healing presence (see Luke 5:17) and people in large numbers will be healed. That shouldn't surprise us! But even if he does that, it may be that some will be passed over.

God may not choose to heal you. You can only assume that your chronic illness is God's way of getting your attention. The purpose of the thorn in the flesh is to keep us humble. We all need something. So could this be yours? Do people say to you, 'Why are you always unwell?' Let us say you feel uncomfortable because you were afraid they thought it, and now they actually say it. People can be so insensitive. Some will say, 'Where's your faith?' Or they may say, 'You're not really that unwell, are you? You're just putting it on. You're just trying to draw attention to yourself. You're wanting sympathy. You can do more for yourself than you're doing. You don't need to be like that!' Or perhaps they say, 'Maybe there's sin in your life, what is God saying to you?' People like this are being like Job's comforters! With friends like that, who needs enemies? 'If you were really right with God', they say, 'you would not be so unwell.' Or they might say to you, 'Are you really trying to get well?'

I admit there are times when there is a connection between illness and one's relationship with God, but I am not talking about that here. I am writing on this subject only with the idea that God has sent this as a means of getting your attention – not because you are wicked, but because it will drive you to know God as a friend. Martin Luther said that we must know God as an enemy before we can know him as a friend.

When I am using terms like 'illness', I always try to consult medical authorities. I am not writing as an expert; I am not a medical person. When I say chronic illness, I could perhaps have called it *chronic disease* or merely *affliction*. Disease can be either acute or chronic. An illness is just the state of being unwell – whether physically, emotionally or mentally. Chronic illness means a disease of long duration involving very slow changes. It is often of gradual onset. It means that it probably won't go away. When there is something chronically unfit about you, it suggests a disease. Disease is a disorder with a specific cause and recognisable symptoms. It could be diabetes, heart trouble, high blood pressure, asthma, allergies, migraines or something even more serious.

I am convinced that one of the best things that happened to me back in 1982 was developing arthritis – and I mean badly. It got so that I couldn't even shake hands with people. It hurt so much that I began to read books on it and then started to eat less red meat, white flour and white sugar for the books suggested that this would help. I remember being in a restaurant in Fort Lauderdale on holiday and explaining the above to the person who was taking us out to eat. Suddenly a lady came over to our table, as only Americans will do, and said, 'Excuse me, sir, I couldn't help but overhear your conversation. Take one teaspoonful of cod liver oil every evening after your last meal before you go to bed for one year, and then once a week thereafter.' I looked at her and thought, who are you? She said, 'Twenty-five years ago, I could not tie my shoes, now look at my hands.' She just walked away. I never saw her again. I'll look her up when I get to heaven, if she's saved; whatever, I was glad of her advice because I decided there was something in what she said and, though I can't stand the taste, I started the cod liver oil in September of 1982 and by April the following year my hands were better. I virtually no longer had the problem – I didn't even get flu or a heavy cold that winter. Since then it has been claimed in various books that a diet of oily fish is good for your heart; so I've been taking cod liver oil all these years, and I am sure it has also had the benefit of keeping my cholesterol level down among other things.

My reason for telling you this is that God has more than one reason in mind when he allows any physical malady. A chronic affliction of any type can keep you humble, and God will get your attention and use you in a way that he couldn't have done otherwise.

I made a couple of phone calls before attempting to write this chapter. I wanted to talk to people who I know

well who have been chronically unfit and unwell. I called
Alex Buchanan. He had an accident years ago; his face
became paralysed, he developed meningitis. He virtually
lost his hearing. He also had a hiatus hernia. I asked Alex,
does all this have anything to do with bringing you closer
to God? He said, 'Has it ever! It's what brought me to
God!' His wife Peggy, who Alex is always pushing in a
wheelchair, has multiple sclerosis. Just imagine the two of
them together. Talk about chronic affliction – it's a
double dose! Alex Buchanan has a wonderful ministry.
If I am in trouble, I often call him. God has used him
powerfully in our lives.

As I mentioned above, a number of years ago my wife
Louise had an ear problem as a result of an accident in
Florida; she punctured her eardrum and developed
tinnitus to the degree that she could hardly hear in that
ear. But when we came back from holiday, on our first
Sunday back in Westminster Chapel, she sat next to
Judith, who is deaf. In that moment Louise wondered if
she should learn sign language. Before then, she had 'put
out a fleece': 'Lord, do you really want me to learn sign
language?'[1] That day she knew. Then she read books on
it, but thought, 'I'm too old to learn', even though she
took a test to see whether she was someone who could
qualify. She only got two out of twenty in the test, so she
thought, 'I guess I'm not supposed to.' She decided
instead to write to a body called Breakthrough, an
organisation that tries to integrate deaf people with
hearing people, and asked if she could take its course.
On the very day she received the application form, she
got a letter from Alex Buchanan. Alex wrote, 'I've been

praying for you, and God has told me that you have come up with something on your own that you feel the Lord would have you do. This is not from your husband, this isn't anyone suggesting it, this is just something that God wants you to do and I am telling you it is from him – go for it!'

My point is, God used this affliction with Louise. But here is Alex Buchanan listening to God and he writes her a letter! You may say, 'Oh, I would like to have a relationship with God like that!' I've got news for you: God wants you to have a relationship with him like that. What will it take to get our attention so that we will spend the necessary time with him, so that he gets to know us and can trust us with that kind of intimacy?

I then phoned Di Parsons. Rob and Di Parsons have a wonderful ministry, a nationwide ministry called Care for the Family.[2] It is now international. Rob is becoming a household name among Christians in America and Canada. They will both tell you that they would not have this today were it not for Di's illness. She has been chronically unwell with ME (also known as chronic fatigue syndrome) for years and they trace their usefulness largely to that. By the way, do you thank God for your good health? I thank him for mine. I have been at Westminster Chapel since January 1977, and I've not missed a Sunday. I can only recall missing a preaching engagement one Friday night, and perhaps a couple of Saturdays when I had to stay in from the Pilot Light ministry when I wasn't feeling too well. God has been so good to me. Do you thank him for your good health?

Jesus cared about the sick. One of the first things said

about Jesus in the New Testament is, 'Jesus went throughout Galilee, teaching in their synagogues, preaching the good news of the kingdom, and healing every disease and sickness among the people' (Matt. 4:23). The sick came to him, and that was much of his ministry. Many might have thought when he died on the cross, 'Oh, what a pity that we are going to lose this wonderful person who can heal.' That could have been one reaction because he healed everybody who came to him. He didn't turn anybody away, he healed them all. But after he died on the cross, rose from the dead, and went to heaven, the ministry of healing continued. It is even mentioned in the very last chapter of the book of Acts that the apostle Paul healed people on the island called Malta. The sick people came to him; he placed his hands on them and healed them, and everybody on the island was cured (Acts 28:9). James says, 'Is any one of you sick? He should call the elders of the church to pray over him and anoint him with oil in the name of the Lord. And the prayer offered in faith will make the sick person well; the Lord will raise him up. If he has sinned, he will be forgiven' (Jas. 5:14–15). Why did James say that? The healing ministry of Jesus was not over. God cares about whether we are well; he still wants to heal.

Is there a connection between illness and sin? How many of us ask, when we do get ill in some way, 'What have I done?' Di Parsons said that the main thing she has had to cope with is this: 'The feeling of what have I done? What have I done to cause this?' We all fear that we've done something wrong and God has 'got it in for us'.

157

And yet in ancient Israel that idea was a very common assumption. Job's 'friends' held to the common jargon, language of Zion in Israel at the time, that if you are suffering, there is sin in your life. They just believed that. So Job was suffering and he said, 'I am sorry, I don't know what I've done!' Job's friends kept coming to him – probing him and probing him – and he would keep saying, 'I don't know what it is,' and they would say, 'You *do* know!' This is the way they thought at the time. In John 9, there is a man blind from birth: 'His disciples asked him, "Rabbi, who sinned, this man or his parents, that he was born blind?" "Neither this man nor his parents sinned" said Jesus, "but this happened so that the work of God might be displayed in his life" ' (John 9:2–3). That reply shows a departure from the ancient way of thinking.

Sometimes sin and suffering *are* related. Sometimes they are so related that James actually said, if one has sinned (meaning that if the illness they are praying for is traceable to sin),[3] when the prayer of faith is offered, then the one who is healed will also have this sin forgiven. So James is showing the *possibility* of the connection with sin. This is why he says 'if' he has sinned, one will be forgiven. And that's a big 'if' because it is implying that sin may not be the cause of illness at all. Do not let the devil accuse you or make you believe that your illness is because of sin. However, if you have a valid suspicion that it is, then, before God, ask for the elders of your church to pray for you. I would even suggest that you confess your sin to them. It might be embarrassing to do so, but that will show that you really want to get well. If you say, 'I have reason to believe that I am in this condition because I haven't really forgiven so-and-so or I have been in a relationship that's not right, or whatever, and God is dealing with me', tell people you trust. If you think there is a connection between your illness and sin, share it with those who will tell no one. That is part of the meaning of James 5:16a: 'Therefore confess your sins to each other and pray for each other so that you may be healed.' It doesn't have to be to the elders or a minister or priest; it is important not that the world knows, but that *somebody* else knows. I am only saying that if there is that suspicion, that is what you can do.

The best people on earth, in whom there is no serious sin at all, have been ill. You should know that God lovingly allows illness and the reason probably is that he wants to get your attention. So do not say to someone, 'There's something spiritually wrong with you!' Jesus said, 'He causes his sun to rise on the evil and the good, and sends rain on the righteous and the unrighteous' (Matt. 5:45b). 'I have seen something else under the sun: The race is not to the swift or the battle to the strong, nor does food come to the wise or wealth to the brilliant or favour to the learned; but time and chance happen to them all' (Eccles. 9:11). Being a Christian isn't going to make you exempt from being ill. Being godly is not going to make you exempt from being ill. Some of God's best have always been unwell.

My Grandma McCurley was a godly woman. Many years ago, before I sold vacuum cleaners, I worked for a life insurance company. My grandmother was seventy at the time and getting too old to get an insurance policy.

But they said that if she was willing to pay the premium, she could still have an insurance policy despite being seventy. So I began to fill out an application form, took her name, date of birth, and all such details. Are you in good health? She replied, 'Yes!' Ever had diabetes? 'Yes!' Ever had high blood pressure? 'Yes!' Have you ever had heart trouble? 'Yes!' Ever had trouble with the gall bladder? 'Yes!' Ever had trouble with the pancreas? 'Yes!' Ever had cancer? 'Yes!' She had had nearly everything you could have. Well, they wouldn't issue the policy, and she died when she was ninety. But she was unwell all of her life.

Paul said to Timothy, 'Stop drinking only water, and use a little wine because of your stomach and your frequent illnesses' (1 Tim. 5:23). So Timothy was obviously unwell quite a lot. Hezekiah was ill to the point of death, and then God gave him fifteen more years (2 Kgs. 20:6). I have always been fascinated by those words in 2 Kings 13:14: 'Elisha suffered from the illness from which he died.' You see, we all have to die. God will also let us become ill and, perhaps, for a long time.

What about illness and stress? Many illnesses are stress-related. I think an interesting medical study could be done on Timothy. Paul said to Timothy, 'For God did not give us a spirit of timidity, but a spirit of power, of love and of self-discipline' (2 Tim. 1:7). Why did Paul say this to him? Timothy was a fearful person. You can see it in 1 Corinthians 16 when Paul urges the Corinthians to be good to Timothy, not to be hard on him because he was apparently a fragile person (1 Cor. 16:10ff), probably motivated largely by a spirit of fear.

There is then a connection between anxiety, fear, stress and being ill. Sometimes there is successful treatment for things like this. But in some cases they may indeed be one's 'thorn in the flesh'. Many physical illnesses are traceable to stress, like indigestion or ulcers. Stress is one of the well-known contributory causes of high blood pressure, which can eventually lead to heart disease. It is like a chain: if enough stress is put on either side, the chain will break at the weakest link. We all have a weak link in our psychological chain. One of my weak links is stress. I sometimes don't sleep well, and then if I go a few days without good sleep I get a sore throat. So stress can cause illness.

Emotional illness is traceable largely to anxiety. Psychologists say that anxiety or depression is the common denominator of all psychopathology. Depression may be a chronic illness. Sometimes depression is the result of a chemical imbalance and may need treatment with drugs. Even so, it may be one's 'thorn in the flesh' if one continually needs medical treatment. This would likely be true in the case of post-natal depression, which sometimes can linger for a good while. A psychosis (a state when you are out of touch with reality) is a far more serious problem, and is often aggravated by stress. That is what William Cowper, the poet and hymn writer, had. He had times when he was completely detached from reality. He would probably be diagnosed as schizophrenic today.

There are also neurotic illnesses – some people seem to welcome illness. Some individuals imagine (or are convinced) that they are ill when they are not. If you tell them they are not ill, they get angry with you. There are also those who, for whatever reason, don't feel safe unless other people think they are unwell. It is a kind of defence mechanism when people enjoy being ill. I recall the time when a filling fell out of my tooth, but after three weeks I found myself enjoying sticking my tongue in the hole in that tooth. It became fun. At first I thought this was awful, and then had to go to the dentist about something else. The dentist said, 'Oh, you've got a hole here in this tooth, so I'll fill it!' I said, 'Oh, don't fill the hole, I love that!' I had got used to it. It is rather like the leaning tower of Pisa. A number of years ago the City Fathers in Pisa in Italy were warned that the tower was going to fall over. They didn't want to correct the tilt, however, for if they made the tower straight again, the tourists wouldn't come. So they wanted to keep it exactly as it was – just not let it get any worse. That's like many of us with an illness. We don't want it to get worse, but we don't really want to be well either in case people ask us to do things for them. They might say, 'You ought to be doing this.' So if we have an excuse, we like to hang on to it.

I remember our old friends Mae and Jess. Jess was one of the best friends I ever had. Both are now in heaven. Jess used to say to me that he could not remember one day in his marriage when at the beginning of the day, Mae would not say, 'Jess, I'll not make it through this day! I am so unwell.' You could go up to her any day of the week and say, 'Mae, I am not feeling well. I didn't sleep too well last night.' She would say, 'Honey, I didn't sleep a wink all night!' Or I would say, 'Mae, I've got a little tummy bug!' She would say, 'My dear, I haven't been able to hold down food for two days!' Whatever you had, she had it – only much worse! She lived to a ripe old age. But there are people like that and they get upset if you suggest that they are not really unwell. I used to think when Mae died they should put on her tombstone, 'See, I told you I was sick!'

But there are illnesses that are certainly not stress-related. I am not trying to explain all these problems, but whatever the reason – whether it's a neurotic, emotional or physical problem – if it hasn't gone away, ask why it hasn't. It just may be that God is graciously trying to get our attention. He is no respecter of persons. You may not have an international ministry like Rob and Di Parsons, or Alex and Peggy Buchanan, but there are thousands who we never hear of who have developed an intimacy with God as a result of their chronic illness. And they wouldn't lose this intimacy for anything in the world.

I want now to deal with illness and submission. That means submitting to God; you come to terms with things. You come to terms with the fact that your illness is not likely to change. That hurts. You keep praying that it will go away – and there is nothing wrong with praying for it to go away. The fact is that Paul said, 'I prayed three times' (2 Cor. 12:8). As I said earlier, you may have prayed more than three times, and that is fine. But at the same time God may be trying to give you a hint. I myself have had to come to terms with some of the most painful things, things I can't write about openly. I repeat, certain things are not likely to change.

Yet you still pray, 'Please take it away!' What do you do then if you still have your illness? You say, 'Yes, Lord!' I will refer to Di Parsons again. She said that the verse that has meant so much to her is when Shadrach, Meshach and Abednego said, 'If we are thrown into the blazing furnace, the God we serve is able to save us from it, and he will rescue us from your hand, O king. But even if he does not, we want you to know, O king, that we will not serve your gods or worship the image of gold you have set up' (Dan. 3:17–18). Take on board the fact that God is able to heal you; he may heal you. But if he doesn't, submit – 'Yes, Lord.' If you've got a back problem, submit. Migraines, submit. Asthma, mental illness, emotional illness, whatever the illness, submit. Be like Job who had to say to those who secretly suspected, 'There is something badly wrong here', 'Though he slay me, yet will I hope in him' (Job 13:15).

I turn now to illness and the possibility of service. That means going to work and also doing something for God. After all, there are some people chronically ill who work forty hours a week. Others have problems far more serious; some are bed-ridden, others are housebound but can still cope. Obviously Paul, who had an eye problem, kept going since it was because of that that he first came to the Galatians. God can cause your illness to coalesce with an event, situation or place wherein you would think, 'I am actually glad I had that illness otherwise this wouldn't have happened!'

Two of the greatest ministries in Westminster Chapel at the moment came into being as a result of Louise's physical problems: our deaf ministry and our prayer ministry. As we have already seen, the deaf ministry wouldn't have happened without Louise's ear problem. Our prayer ministry, through which we have seen some people healed and countless others blessed and refreshed, wouldn't have happened but for Louise suffering severe depression for several years. It was because of chronic illness that she was open to letting anybody pray for her. It's easy to criticise a particular person's ministry, but when you feel ill enough, you'll say, 'If they can heal me, I would like them to pray for me.' That's why we brought in Rodney Howard-Browne.[4] The result of this is that we have a prayer ministry. Whatever condition God has brought to you, he is trying to get your attention – it's the only way he got our attention. If it weren't for William Cowper's illness, we would not have this hymn, surely one of the top five in all church history:

> God moves in a mysterious way,
> His wonders to perform;
> He plants His footsteps in the sea
> And rides upon the storm.

God may use you in his service because of illness. He may turn you into one of the great intercessors of history. You may have a ministry of praying for people, and in heaven – though no one knew you on earth – you could be at the front of the queue to get God's 'Well done!'

This therefore brings me to the subject of illness and spirituality. We are back to that word *intimacy*. God wants your company; he loves your company. 'Me? I can't preach. I can't play a guitar, I can't compose hymns, he wants *me*?' Yes. The most insignificant person whom no one has any time for, God wants. If this chronic illness is not going to go away, why don't you just say, 'Lord, show me what you want?'

There is another reason God gives this chronic illness – perhaps the reason Elisha suffered for a while with an illness before he died – and that is to develop in us a spirituality without being self-righteous. Elisha had seen people healed, and now he was ill. This was possibly so that he too wouldn't be exalted above measure. I feel I must stress this about very spiritual people. I don't mean *superficially* spiritual – I refer to those who are very, very spiritual and very unusual. They have in common that they are not self-righteous. In fact, the most spiritual people are the least self-righteous. Self-righteous people lack spirituality. Do you know why? Because they know that it took something like illness to get their attention. How could they boast? How could they boast about how spiritual they are when they know what God had to do to get their attention?

Is it going to take an illness for you to listen to God and talk to him? Any illness, therefore, is for a reason. A chronic illness – whether you want to call it disease or affliction – is God's way of doing us a favour. Satan will exploit it; he will accuse, he will make you blame yourself. All you now have to do is to confess your sins and walk in the light (1 John 1:7). You must point to the blood of Jesus and say, 'God, you have let this happen to keep me humble.' Not because you have done anything sinful, but it does mean you needed it. We all need something. In your case, this is what it took. This is his will.

10

Personality problems

We all have a thorn in the flesh, perhaps more than one. I am sure that one of them, for many of us, is having a personality problem. However, I have some doubt as to whether I should deal with this, and here is my fear. Because we are dealing with something that is not likely to go away, since Paul said, 'Three times I prayed that it would leave and it didn't', we may conclude that our personality problem is here to stay and therefore have no motivation to deal with it. We might excuse ourselves and say, 'Well, that's just me, that's just me, I will always be like that, always have been, always will be.' For that reason, I wondered if I should deal with it.

Yet I feel I should for this reason. Having a personality problem is, for not a few, a real thorn in the flesh. And in the same way that if your thorn is an unhappy marriage, then it doesn't mean you don't want to do something about it, or if your thorn is chronic illness then it doesn't mean you won't ask for prayer to be healed, so if one's thorn is a personality problem, then surely we would want to do something about it.

As I write these lines, I want you to know I do not

come with the perfect psychological profile. I have so many rough edges; I need much improving and I am working on it all the time. So I hope you don't sense, 'Ah, he's showing us how to be!' We're all in this together.

It is sobering to realise that *you* may be a thorn in the flesh to someone else. Because of your particular personality, has it dawned on you that you are another person's problem? The problem is of course yours, but you unfortunately make it somebody else's as well. It may be the person who has to live with you or work with you, or deal with you from time to time. They regard you as their thorn. You wish you would change. They wish you would change. You force that person to have to walk on eggshells around you. They lose sleep because of you. How does that make you feel? Well, it sobers me to my fingertips, knowing that I may very well be another person's thorn in the flesh.

Perhaps you are aware of your problem, but you say, 'I can't get help, I will always be the same.' People who know you have to accept you the way you are. You are very self-conscious about it, you wish you were different. You've prayed about it often. But have you really tried to get help? We are never too old to learn as long as we want our problems solved. Alas, most of us only want them understood!

We all have rough edges in our personalities. We all want to be liked, want to be accepted by others. There is something in each of us that we wish weren't there. John Calvin said, 'In every saint there is something reprehensible.' That may not necessarily be a personality problem, but it often is.

I often wonder about Jesus and his disciples and his patience with their peculiar personality problems. Peter, James and John went with Jesus up on to a high mountain, and Moses and Elijah appeared before them, talking with Jesus. Then comes the most impertinent, odd, out-of-place comment that could be made. 'Peter said to Jesus, "Lord, it is good for us to be here. If you wish, I will put up three shelters – one for you, one for Moses and one for Elijah" ' (Matt. 17:4). What a dumb thing to say. But there are those of us who are always sticking our foot into it. I have often thought that, when revival comes, Peter's foolish comment will be recalled. For when the Lord's glory is unveiled, people will still make stupid statements.

Then there was Thomas, who wasn't present when the risen Jesus appeared to the disciples. They said to him, 'Thomas, we have seen the Lord!' Now I am aware that the traditional way of looking at Thomas is to say that he was filled with unbelief. After all, he said, 'Unless I see the nail marks in his hands and put my finger where the nails were, and put my hand into his side, I will not believe it' (John 20:25). But I question whether Thomas was filled with sheer unbelief. I honestly believe that Thomas was just hurt that he wasn't there. He knew they weren't making up that story, but he was hurt. He thought, 'I want it to happen to me!' In a way he was saving face: 'Unless I see the nail marks in his hands!'

There was the time when Mark deserted Paul and Barnabas on a particular mission, but when it was time to go on another journey Barnabas wanted to take Mark, and Paul said, 'No!' There followed such a sharp disagreement that Paul and Barnabas parted company (Acts 15:36–9). They just didn't speak. But somebody had to be wrong. Most of us would take Paul's side because we are so conditioned to think that Paul could do no wrong. He later affirmed Mark (2 Tim. 4:11), which of course could mean that Mark changed. My only point is, personality problems get in the way. Why didn't Mark stay with them? Why would Barnabas want him to come? Why couldn't Paul give him a second chance?

For those of us who love Paul, we may want to defend him. But we are told that Ananias the High Priest ordered those standing near Paul to strike him on the mouth. Now that wasn't a very nice thing to do. But here was Paul's opportunity to be like Jesus and inwardly pray, 'Father forgive them, they know not what they do.' Or be like Stephen who said, 'Lord, lay not this to their charge.' But sadly, 'Then Paul said to him, "God will strike you, you whitewashed wall! You sit there to judge me according to the law, yet you yourself violate the law by commanding that I be struck!" ' (Acts 23:3). It was not Paul's finest hour.

There will always be conflicts – personality conflicts. I have often thought that many theological controversies in the history of the Christian Church had little to do with theology – and that a good PhD thesis could be written on how, if you got behind the theological controversies, personality problems governed the outcome. Most people don't bother to see that there were jealousies; many leaders were rivals. The well-known

Puritans John Cotton and Thomas Hooker (founder of the state of Connecticut), both in Boston at first, had contrasting theologies, but they were also rivals. We don't often see this, especially if they are revered people. We just imagine they were godly, that they were wanting the honour and glory of God. It is so often a rival spirit. It is often a fragile ego, jealousy, where somebody just gets under someone else's skin, and can't get along with a particular person.

May I suggest that if people say much the same thing about you (you are insecure, jealous, easily hurt, or whatever), consider it is probably true, that you do have a personality problem. I am not suggesting that you don't love the Lord, or that you are not wanting to please him with all your heart, soul, mind and strength. It is simply that your particular personality problem is most likely to be a thorn in the flesh.

What, then, is a personality problem? It is continued awkwardness in relationships. We all have one (or more) of these problems to some degree. Only Jesus had the perfect personality. He also had the perfect combination of self-confidence and care for others. That is the ideal person: having the balance of self-confidence and concern, care for others. Where there is a lack of this balance, you find a personality that is either very shy and easily offended, or a person who doesn't care for others. The latter can speak very bluntly and frankly, and doesn't bother to examine how it's being received.

So when you don't have a balanced personality, you have difficulty in getting on with people. You keep sticking your foot in it. You keep rubbing people up the wrong way. Perhaps you have trouble making friends or keeping friends, for after a while they get to know you and say, 'I'm not sure I want to be that close to a person like this', and they actually avoid you. You get mad at them, and they don't have the heart to tell you the real problem.

Often you may wish that awkward person would come to you and say, 'Why don't you spend time with me?' You would love to tell them. But they don't do that, and you dare not tell them. And even if they did, you're not sure that they want to know. Somerset Maugham said that when people say they want criticism, they really want praise. How true. But if people generally say much the same thing about you, it is a hint to take it on board. Perhaps you will then put people's backs up less and less.

If this is your thorn in the flesh, you should admit it. Be thankful if you can see it. The worst problem is when you honestly can't see it. So if you think it's awful that you can see it, I can tell you there's one thing worse – and that is *not* to see it. I have people who come to me and say, 'I am told that I am like this and I don't believe it for one minute!' I just roll my eyes heavenwards and smile. They don't want to know.

Do you pray about it, but you've still got it? The reason you know it's a thorn is because it humbles you and embarrasses you. You say, 'I can't believe I have done it again!' No matter how spiritual or close to God you get, it's still there. It doesn't mean you are not a Christian or that you don't love the Lord. But sadly, it could be why you don't have a wider usefulness in God's kingdom. All because you are a difficult person to get on with. The irony is that often people like this are spiritual, by which I mean they have a certain intimacy with God. Some even have had great experiences with God. But if they are not careful, they will take those experiences with God to mean that they are perfectly OK. So Paul said, 'Because of my surpassingly great revelations there was given me a thorn in the flesh' – to compensate, so one won't be conceited. Was a personality problem Paul's own thorn? Who knows?

To what extent is a personality problem a sin? Let us look at the degree to which this is sin and the degree to which it is merely a facet of someone's personality. In other words, at what point does this personality problem become a sin? At what point is it unavoidable, and therefore not necessarily a sin? This is not an easy question to answer. There's a fine line between sin and behaviour that is the result of a deep hurt that has gone on for many years. A personality problem is not necessarily sin. It is because we are sinners that we have it; yes, for none of us is perfect. And yet there is a point at which a personality problem becomes sin: when you excuse it and justify it. If you say, 'Well, that's just me', that's when it's sin. It is sinful when we excuse ourselves and do nothing about it.

What are the causes of a personality problem? All I can do now is look at the tip of the iceberg. There will be exceptions to what follows, but it gives a little hint as to why people are like they are. Every person is worth understanding, as Clyde Narramore says. For example, an only child may be more self-centred than most. I was an only child until I was fifteen. I am sure that I've got the same personality as an only child. A person like this likes the limelight, as I have a tendency to do, and that puts other people's backs up. Or take the person who is the oldest child. Have you ever noticed that often the first-born is very serious, doesn't have much sense of humour? That's partly because the parent expected too much of them. They are often easier on the next child, and even easier on the third. But then when you get to the last, the youngest child, it's almost worse than being an only child; because that child is the mother's baby, and she wants to keep him or her young. The child just grows up wanting a lot of attention. Or take a sickly child, or an injured child. They grew up being cared for, cuddled and being given special attention. They want that all the time. In a word: if a child was favoured by a parent or rejected (which is worse), that child will grow up with an unrealistic expectation or a chip on his or her shoulder. Take people who have difficulties with authority figures; it usually goes right back to their relationship with their parents.

We are all the product of yesterday. All behaviour is in some sense caused. This is true even if our behaviour is partly traceable to inherited genetic traits. Unhappy peer relationships as you grow up can also cause a person to be shaped in an unhappy manner. When other children bullied you, you were traumatised and you have never been quite the same; afraid to trust people, you isolate yourself, you just don't speak, don't want to be hurt. Perhaps you weren't good at sport, you lacked self-confidence; perhaps you were good academically, but you lacked self-confidence generally. Perhaps a school-teacher didn't like you and you blamed yourself, and yet you also have a chip on your shoulder. All these things keep us from growing up, maturing and developing self-confidence.

To put it another way, too little or too much attention as you grew up adversely shapes your personality. It's the way we are made. Some retreat. Some are more outgoing. At the root of a good personality is the right measure of self-confidence. There is a book called *I'm OK, You're OK*. The idea is that the person who has had too little self-confidence grows up with the feeling, 'I'm not OK, but you're OK.' The person who has had too much self-confidence grows up saying, 'I'm OK, but you're not OK.' But the balanced personality is the one who says, 'I'm OK, you're OK.'

A personality problem will almost always manifest itself in some form of manipulation. The word 'manipulate' in this context means when you use or control people and treat them as things rather than human beings. There are basically two kinds of manipulating: active and passive. The active is obvious: he or she comes on strong, twists arms, rather like the high-pressure salesman with an awful lot of confidence. Before you know it, you've agreed to do this; you've been manipulated. The active manipulator is seen in domineering personalities. The passive manipulator is not so easy to spot. You need to learn that nearly everybody is going to manipulate others in one way or another. How does the passive manipulator manipulate? He or she may go quiet. They sulk. They do it in a subtle way, but they still get

what they want. Learn to see this in yourself – accept that
you may be like this. Being the passive manipulator, if
that is what you are, will be harder to see because you
sincerely don't think that you are like that.

Let me give some examples of how we put people off.
Take sulking, when we go quiet. It is forcing somebody
else to say, 'Are you all right?' so that you respond, 'Yes,
I'm fine . . . I'm fine!' We sometimes begin to weep in
order to get a response. There would be no tears if
another person weren't there, for if you were alone you
wouldn't be doing it. It is manipulation. That was what
Mary was like. Jesus came to the tomb of Lazarus; Martha
got up and went, and Mary just stayed behind, sulking
(see John 11:17–32). We may sulk because we are hurt,
or really disappointed like Thomas. He was simply hurt
that he didn't see Jesus, so he then builds up his ego and
says, 'Well, I just want to see the nail prints.' We can say
things like that so easily, and yet we only want to be
understood. But some of us don't see it. It becomes a
lifestyle and, when we are the sulking type of person,
after a while people just don't want to be around us and
God can't use us very widely.

Let's take the hyper-sensitive person. Here is one so
used to getting their feelings hurt, they go down the
street saying, 'I wonder who is going to hurt me today.'
You're ready for it, you just know you are going to get
hurt, you are so used to it; so you've got your defences
up, you live within a frame of mind where you almost
want to get hurt. The person who is so used to being
the object of racial prejudice is always expecting it. You
are more sensitive than anybody else on that subject. If

you were a Greek Jew in the days of the early Church, you felt second-class. You may say, surely a Jew is a Jew. No! Not as they saw it. There were the Hebrew Jews who grew up in Jerusalem or Galilee. They were first-class. Those who had been scattered, they were Greek Jews. The latter were always ready to get their feelings hurt. 'In those days when the number of disciples was increasing, the Grecian Jews among them complained against those of the Aramaic-speaking community [Hebraic Jews] because their widows were being over-looked in the daily distribution of food' (Acts 6:1). No doubt it was true, but the Greek Jews picked up on it quickly.

Then there is the overly scrupulous person. They are overly conscientious even in small matters, so afraid that they won't come up to standard. They are motivated by a spirit of fear. Paul said to Timothy, 'For God did not give us a spirit of timidity, but a spirit of power, of love and of self-discipline' (2 Tim. 1:7). Are you motivated by fear? Are you afraid that you will never please people? Therefore you are overly scrupulous, overly conscientious, and you try too hard in getting it right. People like this don't ever think that they please God.

Another personality problem is the sanctimonious person, the one who makes a show of righteousness. Paul said with biting sarcasm, 'No doubt there have to be differences among you to show which of you have God's approval' (1 Cor. 11:19). There are those who want you to know as early as possible that they have God's approval and how much they love the Lord. As soon as you start talking, they want to talk about the Lord, and you feel it is all for show. I used to know a lady who could not speak without saying something that pointed to how godly she was. She wanted to impress you. I remember one day when I hoped she had changed, I said, 'How are you?' 'I am wonderful today, I am just feeling great!' I thought, 'Oh good, she has changed.' But no sooner than I said that she added, 'And everything is fine with Jesus! Don't you love our Saviour?' All show. You say, 'God bless you!' And they say, 'He does!'

But oftentimes this is to cover some sense of guilt. Frequently people who are so keen to impress you about how godly they are, are often covering something up. Robert Burns put it:

> O wad some power the giftie gie us,
> to see ourselves as others see us.

Robert Burns meant that it is a great thing if God will give you presence of mind so you actually see yourself as others do. Oh, it may hurt! You may think, is that really the way they see me?

Then there is the snob. That is the person who has an exaggerated respect for social position, wealth, certain attainments or taste. The snob doesn't want to mix with people whom he or she regards as inferior. God does not like that. If you want to know how much he doesn't like it, I must remind you that that is the reason some died, some were weak, some were ill following the Lord's Supper in Corinth. When the well-to-do took over and the poor were treated as second-class, God rolled up his sleeves and said, 'Not at my Son's supper you don't!' (See 1 Cor. 11:17–32.) Snobs gravitate only towards those who will make them look good. The relationships they form are superficial and contrived.

You may say, 'But surely this is sin, this is just carnal pride.' No doubt this is true. People like this fear that they won't be admired. Try to sympathise. It's their way of getting their egos stroked. They won't be admired if they are not seen with a certain kind of person. But are we not all like that to some degree?

At the other end of the spectrum is the servile person, one who is excessively submissive. He or she lacks independence. They lack self-confidence. Barak was like this (see Judg. 4:4–16). Deborah came to him with the word of the Lord to conquer the enemy. But Barak said, 'If you don't go with me, I won't go!' Deborah replied, 'If that's the way you want it to be, that's fine but the glory will go to a woman.' Barak didn't care, he didn't mind. People like this usually have no sense of autonomy. Sadly, they may think it is a sign of being humble, but it has absolutely nothing whatever to do with humility. It is often their way of trying to please people – being excessively available, serving. It is sometimes a way to get attention, by trying too hard to please.

Another category of personality problem is the very strict person. It is just as it sounds. Such people require everybody to come up to their standard. Whereas Proverbs 19:11 says, 'A man's wisdom gives him patience; it is to his glory to overlook an offence', a person like this cannot do the latter. If they see something wrong, they feel they must step in because nobody else is going to notice it if they don't. They go in with their sleeves rolled up! It's either black or white. People like this are often pointing the finger. Always moralising, seldom gracious. They wonder why people back off from them.

Then there is the suspicious person, who mistrusts everyone's motives. David said, 'And in my dismay I said, "All men are liars" ' (Ps. 116:11). People like this are afraid to become close to anyone lest they get hurt again. People with a bit of money or prestige don't form friendships because they think they are only wanted because they are famous or rich. The result is that they are lonely.

Take the slanderers. They are only comfortable in a relationship when they are running somebody down. Have you ever seen somebody like that in action? You walk up to two people and if you were able to eavesdrop on that conversation, you would know (and not be surprised) that they are talking about somebody and saying something negative. 'A gossip betrays a confidence; so avoid a man who talks too much' (Prov. 20:19).

Remember this rule of thumb, if people gossip *to* you, they will also gossip *about* you. But there are those who think it is the easiest way to make a friend. I have known cases in which someone, in order to get in with a complete stranger, will say something like 'Do you know what's wrong with this place? Let me tell you what's wrong with these people here!' And another person says, 'Yes, tell me!' They always love it if somebody is going to say something negative. You feed on each other's pathology. Speaking in a negative way is what some relationships are built on.

Then there is the stormy person, who is volatile,

having extreme mood swings from one day to another. You are afraid to see them. You wonder, what kind of mood are they going to be in today? If they are happy you think, 'Oh, it's nice to be around them', but if they are in a bad mood you think, 'I am getting out of here!' 'A hot-tempered man must pay the penalty; if you rescue him, you will have to do it again' (Prov. 19:19).

The above are examples of why some people can't make friends and are always sticking their foot in it.

The key in many cases is the tongue, and this is where it becomes a spiritual or moral problem. We are responsible for what we say:

> When we put bits into the mouths of horses to make them obey us, we can turn the whole animal. Or take ships as an example. Although they are so large and are driven by strong winds, they are steered by a very small rudder wherever the pilot wants to go. Likewise the tongue is a small part of the body, but it makes great boasts. Consider what a great forest is set on fire by a small spark. The tongue also is a fire, a world of evil among the parts of the body. It corrupts the whole person, sets the whole course of his life on fire, and is itself set on fire by hell (Jas. 3:3–6).

A personality problem could eventually become a spiritual problem because we are responsible for what we say. There are those who, if they can't control, will have no relationship. You know you are not going to be friendly with this person because they want to control you. They wonder why people avoid them. There are those who, if

they can't be your closest friend, distance themselves
from you and speak against you. What is God's design in
letting us have a personality problem? As the hymn put it:

> When through fiery trials I call thee to go
> The rivers of woe shall not thee overflow
> The flame shall not hurt thee, I only design
> Thy dross to consume, thy gold to refine.
>
> (Richard Keen, *c.*1787)

I believe this is a thorn we can alter. We don't have to
remain as we are. God sends it to humble us so we must
not justify it. Don't just pray about it. Do something.
Listen to criticism. God gets our attention through a
thorn to help us to see how we could be hurting others
and might be their thorn in the flesh. I would hate to
think I am that to another. I would want to know.

God gets our attention in this way, then, so that we
will listen to others and accept criticism. At the Lord's
Supper we are to examine ourselves (1 Cor. 11:28). As I
said in a previous chapter, when you want to be healed, I
suggest that you confess your faults to the elders. It shows
how deeply you feel about wanting to get things right.
James said that if you do that, you may be healed (Jas.
5:16). In the meantime, accept constructive criticism. Do
you want to solve the problem or only to have it
understood?

God gives us the thorn also to see how a personality
problem can grieve the Holy Spirit (Eph 4:30). If you
really love God, then you won't want to grieve the Holy
Spirit. What we should do is to develop a sensitivity to
the Spirit. We should examine ourselves in the light of

the descriptions I listed above and say, 'Lord, could it be that it's not just other people I am hurting, or it is not just that I am being deprived of wider usefulness, but I am grieving you?'

Paul said, 'Let your conversation be always full of grace, seasoned with salt, so that you may know how to answer everyone' (Col. 4:6). A quick way to overcome personality problems might come if we decided to speak only blessings to people. We will be much further down the line if we speak only blessings. Peter said, 'Finally, all of you, live in harmony with one another; be sympathetic, love as brothers, be compassionate and humble. Do not repay evil with evil or insult with insult, but with blessing, because to this you were called so that you may inherit a blessing' (1 Pet. 3:8–9). Learn to be gracious and accepting. Let people save face. You can win a friend for ever that way. 'Let your gentleness be evident to all' (Phil. 4:5).

Only Jesus had the perfect personality. He had self-confidence, he was never controlling. He cared. Make Jesus your hero. People will be able to tell that this is so. And what is more, the day may come when that thorn just isn't there any more.

> Even though the rain comes down
> It brings life into the ground;
> And I know the sun will shine
> That brings hope into this heart of mine.

> I know God can heal all things
> Broken lives and broken wings;
> Only he can mend a heart
> That this world has torn apart.

Don't look back into the past,
What was fire now is ash;
Let it all be dead and gone,
The time is now for moving on.

As the seasons make their turn,
There's a lesson here to learn;
Broken wings take time to mend
Before they learn to fly again.
On the breath of God they'll soar,
And be stronger than before.

(Janny Grein)

11

Money matters

I do not say that the matter of money was Paul's thorn, but it could have been, for this reason. In Corinth in particular, to work with one's hands as a tentmaker (which Paul had to do) was not something many appreciated. Today many of us would applaud Paul for having the humility to work with his own hands. But to the Greek, anybody who did that was second-class, and they were looked down upon. A philosopher, or anyone who had a brilliant intellect, was one who would never do that, and yet Paul did. It could have been a thorn in his flesh that he had to do such work for a living, especially when it was demeaning to a man of his stature. While at Corinth it was something God told him to do. The Judaisers made themselves look more prestigious to the Corinthians because they commanded large fees. The greater the intellect, the greater the fees one received. Instead of being resented, it was a bonus. People thought more highly of you. The Judaisers capitalised on this and made certain people in Corinth think less of Paul because he took no money from them and worked with his hands. I am not saying that that was his thorn in the flesh, but it is a possibility.

But I do know this, sometimes those who are gifted with unusual revelation are kept poor! I have known some who were most godly, some who were most spiritual, those who got their prayers through to God (if I may put it that way), who have been kept poor.

I can recall that in my old church in Ashland, Kentucky, many years ago, there was one lady who, if you had asked me, was possibly the most godly woman in that church. Everybody also knew that she was poor. Her husband was a drunk, but she was godly. If you had a prayer need, you went to her. I came back from Trevecca College some years later and discovered that her husband had died. Apparently he had a big insurance policy and his widow – this godly woman – was suddenly flourishing financially. But now she was altogether different. The demeanour, the spiritual ethos that used to exude from her, was gone. You didn't go to her any more with prayer requests. It seemed so sad to me.

What I am saying, then, is that there are those who are kept poor and it is for their own good. It is for the good of the Church generally. That doesn't mean that if you are poor, you are godly – or that it is necessarily good to be poor. But I am saying that it could be God's way of keeping you from being conceited. God sends the thorn and allows the devil to walk in as an instrument to achieve a purpose – namely, to keep us humble.

There will be no financial problems in heaven. Why? If only because there will be no tears, no sorrow. There will be no fear; we won't have to work to eat. It will all be laid on, provided throughout eternity. It's hard to believe that that day is coming. But it is coming – it's not far down the road. Heaven will possibly be sweeter in a sense, I would have thought, for some who here below have suffered financially all their lives.

There are of course those who don't ever worry about financial problems. They have got high incomes either by inherited wealth, by hard work, by good education, or through prestigious jobs. They buy what they want, live in nice homes, eat good food. When they get to heaven, I wonder – humanly speaking – if they will be able to appreciate it!

Some have struggled all their lives. They were born poor, remained poor. They get no breaks. They didn't have a secure background. They didn't get a good education. They have struggled all their lives. Heaven, I would have thought, will be sweeter for people like that. I think of the old spiritual:

> You got shoes, I got shoes, all God's children got shoes.
> When I get to heaven I am going to put on my shoes
> And walk all over God's heaven.

The black slaves in Alabama and Mississippi 150 years ago didn't have shoes.

A thorn in the flesh, when it comes to money matters, I define as the continual inability either to get ahead financially or to manage money.[1] No doubt many would say, 'Well, that's me!' I know that some middle-class people have more financial problems than anybody else. Partly because of greed, they never have enough, or partly because they are 'keeping up with the Jones's'.

Sometimes middle-class people set a higher standard for themselves and may be resented by poor people. I know of one individual who lives from hand to mouth (but is in a high-income bracket) because he needs an extra £10,000 a year just to keep his child at a public school. There are people who wouldn't even think of a need like that. But to some, that is a real need. Is that a thorn in the flesh? It could be for someone who is well paid and yet lives from hand to mouth! The thorn in the flesh may be the difficulty in making ends meet, no matter how hard you try.

The subject of money causes some people to became very quiet! Arguably, Jesus had more to say about money than anything else. None the less, we get sensitive about it. Money, to many Christians, certainly in Britain (if I may be forgiven for saying this), is like sex in the Victorian age: everybody thought about it, but never talked about it. That's the way many are with money.

The reason for money problems, generally speaking, is because of the Fall. Adam and Eve sinned in the Garden of Eden and God said to Adam, 'By the sweat of your brow you will eat your food until you return to the ground, since from it you were taken; for dust you are and to dust you will return' (Gen. 3:19). Money doesn't grow on trees; 99 per cent of us have to work for it. And, in theory, in a welfare state no one needs to go without food, shelter or clothing.

Being a Christian doesn't exempt us from the curse of the Fall, and the apostle Paul made himself no exception. He also said to the Thessalonians:

> For you yourselves know how you ought to
> follow our example. We were not idle when we
> were with you, nor did we eat anyone's food
> without paying for it. On the contrary, we
> worked night and day, labouring and toiling so
> that we would not be a burden to any of you.
> We did this, not because we do not have the
> right to such help, but in order to make
> ourselves a model for you to follow. For even
> when we were with you, we gave you this rule:
> 'If a man will not work, he shall not eat' (2
> Thess. 3:7–10).

The Christian faith ought to motivate a person to work. I can give no good reason for a lazy Christian; it doesn't add up. Some say the Puritan work ethic gave rise to the middle class. There's nothing wrong with being middle class so long as the Christian who is middle class is not a snob and doesn't make anybody else feel second-class. That was the danger in Corinth; there were those middle-class people who treated the poor as second-class and that's why God dealt with them severely (1 Cor. 11:17–32). James gave a warning; he said:

> Now listen, you rich people, weep and wail
> because of the misery that is coming upon you.
> Your wealth has rotted, and moths have eaten
> your clothes. Your gold and silver are corroded.
> Their corrosion will testify against you and eat
> your flesh like fire. You have hoarded wealth in
> the last days. Look! The wages you failed to pay
> the workmen who mowed your fields are crying

out against you. The cries of the harvesters have
reached the ears of the Lord Almighty. You have
lived on earth in luxury and self-indulgence. You
have fattened yourselves in the day of slaughter.
You have condemned and murdered innocent
men, who were not opposing you (Jas. 5:1–6).

This warning came not because they were wealthy, but
because they mistreated people. If a money problem is
not your thorn in the flesh today, remember that it could
be tomorrow. God can take it all away from you, just like
that!

Paul said to Timothy:

But godliness with contentment is great gain. For
we brought nothing into the world, and we can
take nothing out of it. But if we have food and
clothing, we will be content with that. People
who want to get rich fall into temptation and a
trap and into many foolish and harmful desires
that plunge men into ruin and destruction. For
the love of money is a root of all kinds of evil.
Some people, eager for money, have wandered
from the faith and pierced themselves with many
griefs (1 Tim. 6:6–10).

Are you that? Do you want to get rich? God in heaven
may be folding his arms and saying, 'Really?' Some
Christians cannot get ahead financially. I am going to
tell you why. God won't let them. He's doing some an
enormous favour. It could destroy them. They already
have trouble handling money and they think, 'Well, if I

had a little more . . .' Almost certainly, if they had a little more they would be deeper in debt. This is the way most of us are. We are by nature greedy. Very few people, truly, can handle money.

The warning about money also comes from John:

> Do not love the world or anything in the world. If anyone loves the world, the love of the Father is not in him. For everything in the world – the cravings of sinful man, the lust of his eyes and the boasting of what he has and does – comes not from the Father but from the world. The world and its desires pass away, but the man who does the will of God lives for ever (1 John 2:15–17).

Jesus said: 'Do not store up for yourselves treasures on earth, where moth and rust destroy, and where thieves break in and steal. But store up for yourselves treasures in heaven, where moth and rust do not destroy, and where thieves do not break in and steal. For where your treasure is, there your heart will be also' (Matt. 6:19–21).

The man I was named after, R.T. Williams, told the story of a millionaire who gave $100,000 to the Church of the Nazarene. The man then went bankrupt. Everybody went to him and said, 'Well, now how do you feel, you gave all that money to God. Wouldn't you like to have it back?' 'Oh no,' he said, 'That's the only amount I kept!' Store up for yourselves treasures in heaven.

There are some Christians who would have the breakthrough of breakthroughs were they to become detached from money and material things:

Therefore I tell you, do not worry about your life, what you will eat or drink; or about your body, what you will wear. Is not life more important than food, and the body more important than clothes? Look at the birds of the air; they do not sow or reap or store away in barns, and yet your heavenly Father feeds them. Are you not much more valuable than they? Who of you by worrying can add a single hour to his life? And why do you worry about clothes? See how the lilies of the field grow. They do not labour or spin. Yet I tell you that not even Solomon in all his splendour was dressed like one of these. If that is how God clothes the grass of the field, which is here today and tomorrow is thrown into the fire, will he not much more clothe you, O you of little faith? So do not worry, saying, 'What shall we eat?' or 'What shall we drink?' or 'What shall we wear?' For the pagans run after all these things, and your heavenly Father knows that you need them. But seek first his kingdom and his righteousness, and all these things will be given to you as well. Therefore do not worry about tomorrow, for tomorrow will worry about itself. Each day has enough trouble of its own (Matt. 6:25–34).

My father's favourite verse is Matthew 6:33, 'But seek first his kingdom and his righteousness, and all these things will be given to you as well.' He never became wealthy, but we were never really poor. Perhaps you reach out for those things that are to be added, but you have got it the wrong way around. You may say, 'If I had a little bit more, I'd pray more; if I get this done, I will give more time to God. If I get this which I want, then I am going to start going to church more and reading my Bible more.' Wrong! You will never do it! Seek first the kingdom of God, pursue righteousness and godliness. Take time to be alone with him, then all these other things will just be there! The very things that you wanted, surprisingly, he will give you. God can do that.

The 'thorn' is being oppressed because of money worries. Older people with fixed incomes have no earning power. They are stuck. On the other hand, many young people with a good education can't get a job, and they are in debt. Nothing can rob you of peace of mind like financial worry.

I am the world's expert on this! I have made every mistake that can be made. When it comes to this subject I know what I am talking about. What happened originally was this. I came home from Trevecca College having had visions that God would use me. God told me that I would one day have an international ministry. I just thought that it would happen a month or two later. When I could see it wasn't going to happen as soon as I had hoped, I had to get a job to make ends meet. I remember thinking that the first thing I needed was a new suit, so I got into debt to get this. Then the salesman in the shop said, 'You need a pair of shoes to go with your suit', so I got that. I needed a shirt, two shirts, then three. I got a couple of new ties and socks. I needed a sports jacket as well as a suit. I left that store owing $400, a lot of money back in 1956. Then somebody said, 'How would you like to fly?' 'Yeah, one day, when the ministry comes, I will need to fly – I'll need to fly my own plane.' So a friend of mine sold me a 120 Cessna for $1,700. In the meantime, I had a job selling baby equipment. I went into the bank to borrow some money to buy the plane, and the banker said, 'How much money do you make?' Well, that week I had made three sales so I said, '$150.' 'Oh, that's good, that's $8,000 a year, we can loan you anything you want on that income.' What I didn't tell him was that the previous three weeks I hadn't made a sale at all! By the time I met Louise two years later, I was so deeply in debt that I blush to think about it.

Why did God allow that? I think I know now. It kept me from getting into the ministry for a number of years. But I learned how to handle money, I had made my mistakes. I learned to get to know people. I learned to know business. Finance. I personally think that the worst thing that can happen to many young people is for them to go to theological college or seminary, then go right into the Church, without knowing people, how to handle money, or do business. I am now all the better for it. 'All things work together for good.' I can tell you, I learned my lesson.

There is a difference between needs and wants. 'And my God will meet all your needs according to his glorious riches in Christ Jesus' (Phil. 4:19). The psalmist said, 'I was young and now I am old, yet I have never seen the righteous forsaken or their children begging bread' (Ps. 37:25). It is not always easy to know the difference between our wants and our needs.

These are hard days. It's a difficult era. Today's society encourages debt. My advice, do not go into debt if you can possibly avoid it (a mortgage would be an exception to this). Satan wants you to be in debt because you will be in continuous bondage, continuous worry. You can't worship as you should. You are always worrying about how you are going to succeed and you are preoccupied. I know the problem. I know what it was like to be a young person who dreaded opening the post to read, 'Dear Mr Kendall, We are handing your account over to our solicitors.' Or, 'Mr Kendall, Will you please return your credit card at once or we will come to take it from you.' But they don't do that today. If you go over your credit card limit, you'll get a nice letter saying, 'We have decided to extend the amount you can borrow.' Almost anybody in the world can get a credit card. I was talking to somebody the other day, who doesn't have a job and who said, 'Look here, I've got a credit card, isn't God good!' I thought, 'You think that's God's mercy to you – that particular bank will always do that!' On their books it shows how much money they've got coming in. They don't know they aren't going to get it, but that's the way they are. You've got a £600 limit; now you owe £602, but instead of asking for your credit card, they make it £1,000. You go to £1,015; they go to £1,500. That is today's society. It's wicked.[2]

Don't borrow from friends. That will put a strain on your relationship. Back in Kentucky there were two friends who said, 'You know, we love each other, don't we?' 'We are friends to the end.' 'Right!' One said, 'Loan me $10.' The other said, 'That's the end!' Any time that you borrow from friends will almost always put a strain on that relationship. When someone says, 'It's not the money, but the principle', it's always the money.

For some, 'weakness' and 'money' are words to be used interchangeably. I am not particularly talking about the love of money, although of course that's a weakness. But I am talking about the inability to handle money. Often it's a case of not having been taught. I am not writing this to make anyone feel bad or guilty, but I have to say that the reason most people don't tithe is because they haven't been taught. Go to a church where they don't tithe, and you will find nearly every time that the minister doesn't teach it. The same is true when it comes to handling money. Such people didn't get the importance of handling money well drummed into them from childhood. The ability to handle money well can often make what you have go three times further.

I have often been amazed at people who live on state benefits and yet who go into Sainsbury's or Tesco's and come out with Cokes and crisps and use up all their money. Those things are expensive and then they say, 'I'm hungry.' Other people can take the same amount of money when they shop and buy enough to live on the whole week. Sadly, sometimes poverty goes hand in hand with a lack of education as to what foods are good for you – as well as having a lack of education in how to handle money.

It's called 'living within your income'. Better than that, it's living on 90 per cent. My father taught me this mathematical incredulity – that the 90 per cent goes as far as the 100 per cent, and sometimes even further, when you give God his 10 per cent. But some people with high incomes have this weakness of spending money foolishly. Even when they go into a shop for food, they may over-estimate their ability to pay for things.

Or they may not know how to budget. Why would keeping to a budget threaten people? In much the same way as the person who doesn't want a physical examination because he's afraid there's something wrong with him, and therefore doesn't go at all, so some people avoid having a budget. You can say to a person who is having financial problems, 'Do you budget?' and that individual may feel threatened. Having a budget means that you know how much money is going to come in; you are aware of what is going out.

Learn to plan each day accordingly. Some people are brilliant at doing this. My Grandma McCurley could make money go further than anybody I have ever known. She and her family lived quite well, and yet they were fairly poor. But they made it. They *always* paid the tithe. They were poor, but always paid the tithe; they wouldn't have thought of not doing it. In my old denomination they were mostly poor people, yet almost all tithed.

The inability to handle money probably means you will get into debt. The result is that you always live in fear and justify doing things you know are wrong, saying, 'I can't help it, I've got to eat.' Some are always buying things simply to impress others with their possessions: clothes, car, computer, stereo, etc. They try to impress people that they don't really like that much, so they will think, 'Oh, that's nice.' That is often why it makes you so happy buying something. But it's so stupid. At Christmas, many buy presents for people they don't like, giving them presents they don't want, with money they don't have! The result is that our income and our outgoings are like water going into and out of a bucket with holes in it.

Do you know why? It's God. He controls how much money comes in, and if he can see that you are not going to handle money very well, he will put holes in that bucket. The money comes in and money goes out and you think, 'Where's it all gone?' It's God's way of keeping us humble.

That could change. I honestly believe God would give us more if we would continue to love him and pray as much and resist temptation. I don't think God objects to people being wealthy. But those who can cope with it are few. However, God knows what we are like and some he keeps poor, doing us a great favour. Learn to handle money and establish a pattern of walking in the light, being faithful to God, spending time with him, and wanting to be like Jesus, not having any spirit of bitterness, no vengeance, and God may surprise you with what he will do. But if he knows that it is going to hurt you, he's not going to let you have it. I might add: he's not going to let you win the Lottery. I would like to think that no Christian would support the Lottery. It plays into people's poverty and greed, even letting some fantasise and get deeper into debt – hoping their lucky day will come.

Wisdom in the use of money will be shown by being a thankful person. Do you really thank God for the essential things of life? Do you thank him for your job? Do you thank him for your income? If money matters is not your thorn today, remember it could be your thorn in the flesh tomorrow. For example, that job you have, he could just take it away from you. He could cause the money you have invested in a certain way to be lost in twenty-four hours. Therefore, be thankful that you are not oppressed at the moment by your situation.

My friend Mark Moore actually gives this advice: live on 80 per cent of your income; tithe 10 per cent and save 10 per cent. You may say, 'I can't even live on 90 per cent!' I answer: pull back so that you can. Perhaps you feel you cannot live on 80 per cent at the moment, but the ability to handle money (when we give God all of his) may be a gift you are given that you weren't expecting to have. It is just like Jesus multiplying the loaves and the fish; it doesn't have a natural explanation. It doesn't add up that 90 per cent can go as far as 100 per cent.

In those days when I was so deep in debt, I justified not tithing. I said, 'God knows it is not spiritual to owe this money, and he would want me to pay my debts before I give to him!' I will never forget one day coming home shortly after Louise and I were married. God had hidden his face from me for days and weeks. I hadn't made any sales. I thought, 'Will I ever get to be in the ministry? Whatever happened to those visions that God was going to use me?' My Grandma McCurley had given us a beautiful white Bible. It was lying on the dining room table in this little flat we had in Springfield, Illinois. It was somehow opened to a particular place, but I hadn't noticed where it was opened at. I thought, 'Lord, I am going to walk over to my Grandma's Bible, so please,

please, Lord, let it be something to encourage me!' I walked over to it and, I promise you, my eyes fell right on these words: 'Will a man rob God? Yet you rob me. But you ask, "How do we rob you?" "In tithes and offerings" ' (Mal. 3:8). I abruptly closed that Bible, walked over and turned on the television that we still owed for, and I thought, 'I certainly didn't want a word like that.' Perhaps you feel that way at this moment.

But money matters wasn't always to be my thorn. The day came when God removed it. But I have to say that as a result of not tithing but paying my bills, do you know what? I owed more a year later than I did when I made the decision not to tithe. And a year after that, I owed more. One day I said, 'I will start tithing now!' In eighteen months, we were out of debt.

Tithing is a part of worshipping God. Abraham was the first tither. He gave spontaneously, gratefully, freely – and it pre-dated the Law. These people who quickly dismiss tithing by saying, 'That's being under the Law!' are wrong. Tithing came in before the Law, and now that the Law has been fulfilled in Christ, Abraham is the perfect prototype of the Christian. The gospel was preached to Abraham (Gal. 3:8); he is the prototype of a Christian and he was the first tither.

The only time in the Bible where there is any hint that we ought to prove the existence of God is in Malachi 3:10. In the Middle Ages they had their various proofs of God. Thomas Aquinas came up with the cosmological proof for God and the teleological proof of God. The Bible doesn't actually bother to prove God. The nearest it comes is the way the Authorised Version translates

Malachi 3:10. It says: 'Bring ye all the tithes into the storehouse, that there may be meat in mine house, and prove me now herewith, saith the LORD of hosts, if I will not open you the windows of heaven, and pour you out a blessing, that there shall not be room enough to receive it.' That's in the Old Testament. But listen to the New Testament: 'Remember this: Whoever sows sparingly will also reap sparingly, and whoever sows generously will also reap generously' (2 Cor. 9:6). And: 'Those who honour me I will honour' (1 Sam. 2:30).

We should not give necessarily because a church needs it, although sometimes that is the case; you give because it's right to do so. I do you no favour to withhold this from you, for we are the losers if we are not giving God what is his. I will tell you another reason for my writing in this way. Those who tithe consistently will generally be those who (1) manage money well, (2) live within their income, (3) aren't wealthy, but are contented, happy people, and (4) don't really miss that 10 per cent but find that the 90 per cent goes as far, if not further, than the 100 per cent they kept to themselves.[3]

If money matters is your thorn, it is because God knows you. I used to ask, 'God, why don't you pay my debts so that I can get back into the ministry?' But there was a purpose in it all. And there is a purpose in anybody's financial struggle. God loves you. You are loved with an everlasting love. He cares. The day will come when he will sanctify to you your deepest distress.

Your thorn may not be a thorn for ever. It was temporary for Job, wasn't it? God leaves the thorn there for the moment because it's for our good. Some of God's sovereign vessels were wealthy, like Abraham. So don't be jealous of those who don't have financial worries like you have. You may not always be in your situation. Remember that Paul said, 'But godliness with contentment is great gain' (1 Tim. 6:6). And also: 'Remember this: Whoever sows sparingly will also reap sparingly, and whoever sows generously will also reap generously' (2 Cor. 9:6).

12

An unwanted calling

A thorn in the flesh may be an unwanted calling. That is when what God wants is not what you want. It is what you have to do, though it is the opposite of what you want.

The word 'calling' in the New Testament is used in several ways. Generally speaking, there is *effectual calling*, and there is what I would call *career calling*. Effectual calling is the work of the Holy Spirit in conversion. God does this because we would never be saved if he hadn't done it. So an unwanted calling is even being a Christian! None of us chose to be Christians. Jesus said, 'You did not choose me, but I chose you' (John 15:16). By his Spirit he brought us to the place where we became willing, and we cannot take one bit of credit for that. It is what God did. The word 'called' is used that way on many occasions: 'And those he predestined, he also called; those he called, he also justified; those he justified, he also glorified' (Rom. 8:30); 'And you also are among those who are called to belong to Jesus Christ' (Rom. 1:6); 'Brothers, think of what you were when you were called. Not many of you were wise by human standards;

not many were influential; not many were of noble birth'
(1 Cor. 1:26). Jesus used the word 'chosen'. He said, 'For
many are invited, but few are chosen' (Matthew 22:14).
Now that is because if God didn't do it, we would never
be saved. That's the effectual calling.

But that is not mainly what I am writing about here. I
am referring to career calling, God's plan for your life.
Paul said he was called to be an apostle. For him that
calling came at the point of his conversion. As soon as he
was converted, he was told he was to go to the Gentiles
(Acts 9:15). It was built into his conversion experience.
But some of us discover much later, long after we have
been converted, what God is going to do with our lives.
Some also find that they are not happy with what God is
planning in their lives, because it isn't happening like
they thought it would happen. To Peter and Andrew,
Jesus said, 'Come, follow me . . . and I will make you
fishers of men' (Matt. 4:19). Peter had been a fisherman
and God called him to be a soul winner. It was not
something that Peter had wanted.

There is also a close connection between our natural
gifts and God's calling for life, or career calling. We all
have gifts, but they are not all used in the same way:

Now the body is not made up of one part but of
many. If the foot should say, 'Because I am not a
hand, I do not belong to the body,' it would not
for that reason cease to be part of the body. And
if the ear should say, 'Because I am not an eye, I
do not belong to the body,' it would not for that
reason cease to be part of the body. If the whole

body were an eye, where would the sense of
hearing be? If the whole body were an ear,
where would the sense of smell be? But in fact
God has arranged the parts in the body, every
one of them, just as he wanted them to be. If
they were all one part, where would the body
be? As it is, there are many parts, but one body
(1 Cor. 12:14–20).

Here is a person who wanted to be the head, or the eye;
but he is only the foot or the hand, and he's frustrated.
He wanted to be high profile in the Church. He said,
'God, why can't I be up front where people will see me?'
God says, 'Sorry, you're to be like the small intestines.
You are like the pancreas. You are like those organs in
the body that aren't seen but are very necessary': 'On the
contrary, those parts of the body that seem to be weaker
are indispensable, and the parts that we think are less
honourable we treat with special honour. And the parts
that are unpresentable are treated with special modesty,
while our presentable parts need no special treatment.
But God has combined the members of the body and has
given greater honour to the parts that lacked it' (1 Cor.
12:22–4).

There are those who want to be behind the scenes
and, if you gave them their choice, they would rather be
the 'liver' or the 'kidneys' or the 'lungs' where they are
not seen. But God instead makes them be the eye, the
ear, the head! It is an unwanted calling. It is when God's
plans overrule yours. It is when you have been kept from
doing what you wanted to do and it's frustrating. To be

converted is one thing, but when you are subsequently called to do or be something that you hadn't wanted to do or be, that's quite another. It is having to spend your life doing what by choice you wouldn't have preferred at all – but your talent is best suited for something else. As for your education, it all seems to have gone down the drain. You went to university to study this, and now look at what you are having to do for a living! When it comes to where God has put you, you may feel over-qualified and frustrated. Or you may feel under-qualified and frustrated. It may also be that you are required to work with people you would never have chosen to work with. It may be that you are in a place you would never have chosen to be. You are having to live and work in a place which is the last place on earth you wanted to be.

Could this be a thorn in the flesh? Yes! You have never been happy over the years with the work you've had to do. With the place you've had to work in. With the people you've been put with. It's not even work that you were trained to do. It's not even in the area of your expertise. It's not what you had planned to do, and over the years you have kept thinking this must be going to change: 'I'm not always going to be doing this!' But then the years go by and you are still doing this work. 'I'm not always going to have to be with these people!' Years go by and you're still with them and you keep thinking, 'It will end!' But it hasn't yet. God has led you to where you are, but inwardly you think, 'Surely there must be something better in life for me than this? Is this it? Is this all there is?'

Life is passing you by. You grew up looking forward

to being this or that; maybe a doctor, maybe a lawyer. Maybe you wanted to be a nurse, maybe you wanted to be a computer programmer. Maybe you wanted to work in a particular area and you could even see yourself there. It seems that nothing has gone according to plan.

Could this have been Paul's thorn in the flesh? It could have been. After all, he had to work with his hands after he became a Christian and with a people he had been brought up to believe were second-class: Gentiles. Had he managed to do what he wanted to do, he would have been able to work with his own people. Do you know, as long as he lived, he never got over that? Listen to him:

> I speak the truth in Christ – I am not lying, my
> conscience confirms it in the Holy Spirit – I have
> great sorrow and unceasing anguish in my heart.
> For I could wish that I myself were cursed and
> cut off from Christ for the sake of my brothers,
> those of my own race, the people of Israel.
> Theirs is the adoption as sons; theirs the divine
> glory, the covenants, the receiving of the law,
> the temple worship and the promises. Theirs are
> the patriarchs, and from them is traced the
> human ancestry of Christ, who is God over all,
> for ever praised! Amen (Rom. 9:1–5).

That was where his heart was and he never got over it! He yielded to what God wanted him to do and it was God's built-in plan from the beginning. As soon as he was converted, he was told what he had to do. I wonder how many people are afraid of becoming a Christian because they fear that the moment they become a

Christian God is going to send them to Africa or South America or some other far-flung place. Well, as soon as Paul was converted he had something worse than that – he was sent to the Gentiles. Every Jew in those days thanked God daily that he wasn't a Gentile; that he wasn't a woman; and that he wasn't a dog. 'On the contrary, they saw that I had been given the task of preaching the gospel to the Gentiles, just as Peter had been given the task of preaching the gospel to the Jews' (Gal. 2:7).

Now think about it. Peter is the one who went to the house of Cornelius, having had a dramatic spiritual experience. He was led sovereignly to Cornelius, and saw the Spirit of God coming down on Cornelius, a Gentile (Acts 10:9–48). You would have thought that Peter would be the one to reach Gentiles! If ever there was somebody who was tailor-made for the Jews, it was Saul of Tarsus. He had studied under Gamaliel. Consider the stature of Gamaliel. He was the learned person of the Law in the first century. There was no one like him. What Albert Einstein was to physics, Gamaliel was to the Jewish Law. Paul studied under him and you would have thought, 'Here is one that will reach Jews.' But God said, 'No, I want you to go to the Gentiles.'

To us it just doesn't add up. All his life Paul was looking over his shoulder, trying to reach Jews at every opportunity. He said, 'The gospel is to the Jew first' (Rom. 1:16), and I can tell you, every chance he got, he was talking to a Jew. I am quite convinced this is what eventually got him into real trouble. There is little doubt in my mind that when those people came to him and said, 'Don't go to Jerusalem', they were led of the Spirit (Acts 21:4–11). Luke says, 'By the Spirit they said, "Don't go." ' Paul said, 'I'm going!' He kept thinking that one day, somehow, he was going to convert the Jews. When he went to Jerusalem, it was a big disaster. It didn't happen.

Maybe that's you. You are still hoping somehow to do something else. You say, 'I am not going to do this all my life!' You try to do what God won't let you do, and it just doesn't come off. Paul's lasting success was with the very people he had grown up to think very little of. It was an unwanted calling.

I met a man who became one of David Brainard's biographers, a Harvard man. He probably knew more about David Brainard (1718–47) than anybody. David Brainard was a godly young man who saw many Indians in New York state converted. Had he lived he would have been Jonathan Edwards' son-in-law, but he died at the age of twenty-nine. Jonathan Edwards published Brainard's journal. That journal was once said to have inspired more people to be missionaries than any body of literature next to the Bible. John Wesley (1703–91) said, 'Let all our people read David Brainard's journal.'

That biographer said something to me that I was not prepared for: 'David Brainard did not really like the Indians that he had to witness to in New York state. He actually couldn't bear them!' Yet here was this godly man who became a legend because of his ministry to the American Indians. Now why does God do this?

There is a consistent pattern behind many an un-wanted calling. For example, take an unwanted calling to singleness rather than being married. Could it be that you are one of those who grew up hoping that you would get married? All your life you have fantasised about that perfect woman, that perfect man. You just took for granted that one day you would be married. Now if you are not married at the moment, I do not want you for one minute to think, 'That means I'm not going to get married!' I'm not saying you're not going to get married, I'm just saying that there are those who won't. Jesus' disciples said to him: ' "If this is the situation between a husband and wife, it is better not to marry." Jesus replied, "Not everyone can accept this teaching, but only those to whom it has been given. For some are eunuchs because they were born that way; others were made that way by men; and others have renounced marriage because of the kingdom of heaven. The one who can accept this should accept it" ' (Matt. 19:10–12). It could be that you are one of those to whom God says, 'Stay single.'

The apostle Paul was probably widowed. He was almost certainly a rabbi and a rabbi had to be married. It is believed that when he said, 'I wish that all men were as I am' (1 Cor. 7:7), it probably meant that he was going to be celibate for the rest of his life. He gave this advice: 'I would like you to be free from concern. An unmarried man is concerned about the Lord's affairs – how he can please the Lord. But a married man is concerned about the affairs of this world – how he can please his wife – and his interests are divided' (1 Cor. 7:32–4a). Paul was making a case here for remaining unmarried. So it could be that for some, after all these years, you are having to come to terms with this as being the way God wants it for you.

Take an unwanted calling as to secular involvement. You took subjects at school and later on went deeper into them. Perhaps you read law, or French or medicine. Then when it came to finding a job, none was available in the area of your preparation or training. Perhaps you learned Chinese and now you are working as a secretary. You studied philosophy or theology and you are working as a taxi driver. You went to university and you are working as a salesperson in a department store.

Joseph was bred by his father to be the first-born. That meant special treatment in ancient times including a double share in the inheritance. Joseph wasn't really the first-born; that was Reuben. But Jacob was unhappy with Reuben and turned to Joseph. So Joseph's brothers were jealous of him and they kidnapped him. The next thing you know is that Joseph, who had never worked a day in his life, was now a slave in the house of Potiphar, an Egyptian officer. He must have thought, what on earth is this all about? Talk about an unwanted calling! But the Bible says, 'The Lord was with him.' That is what matters.

Unwanted calling? But is the Lord with you? That matters! The day came when Joseph could say, 'God meant it for good!' Oh, did God ever have plans for Joseph. And God has plans for you. Even if you still don't understand, in heaven you will see that it was the only way God could lead you. When I was a boy I used to hear George Beverley Shea sing:

> We'll talk it over in the bye and by;
> We'll talk it over my Lord and I.
> I'll ask the reason He'll tell me why
> When we talk it over in the bye and by.

God called Paul to be an apostle; he had sophisticated training in the Jewish Law. And yet we find him working as a tentmaker to support himself. It was a demeaning task working with his hands, as we saw above, and it did not impress the first Greek in Corinth. Anybody with Paul's education commanded big fees for their rhetoric and speaking ability. But here was Paul enduring the humiliation of working with his hands. It was in some sense a thorn in the flesh.

Perhaps you felt called to be a foreign missionary and you are still living in your own country and have to work there. Or maybe you have to do a kind of Christian work as plan B – waiting for that more fulfilling opportunity. I had an uncle who felt that God called him to Africa. He and his wife applied to go to Africa through the Foreign Mission Board of their denomination and they waited and waited. In the meantime, they were given a church to pastor. After a few more years they got another church. I can recall my uncle weeping as he talked about Africa and the burden he had for Africa. He never went. Maybe you feel called to the pastorate and you have ended up teaching school. Some settle for being deacons when they thought they would be ministers one day. They are working in the world in secular employment.

One must take into consideration the providence of an

unwanted calling. Perhaps God has given you a mission you didn't ask for. 'By faith Abraham, when called to go to a place he would later receive as his inheritance, obeyed and went, even though he did not know where he was going' (Heb. 11:8).

How's that for trying to impress your friends? 'What are you up to, Abraham?' 'Not sure!' 'What do you mean, not sure, what's happening in your life?' 'Well, I am obeying God!' 'Where are you going?' 'Not sure!' That was it. In fact, 'The LORD had said to Abram, "Leave your country, your people and your father's household and go to the land I will show you" ' (Gen. 12:1). What kind of a mission is that? Yet Abraham became one of the greatest men in all history. He's known as the father of the faithful. He had no idea what it would lead to. Jesus said, 'Whoever can be trusted with very little can also be trusted with much, and whoever is dishonest with very little will also be dishonest with much' (Luke 16:10).

Do you feel that life is passing you by although you've kept your eyes on the Lord? He's led you to this place and to that place, and you can see that he did lead you there, but you think to yourself, 'This is not what I had in mind!' But it's not over yet! There was a lot for Abraham to discover.

What if you are given a mandate you didn't ask for? God said to Jonah, 'Go to the great city of Nineveh and preach against it, because its wickedness has come up before me' (Jonah 1:2). That is what he had to do. He said, 'Oh no! I'm not going to do that!' God said, 'Really?' So while Jonah was on a Mediterranean cruise,

God sent the wind. The only choice of the mariners was to throw him overboard. Then God sent the fish. The same Jonah who prayed he wouldn't have to go, now prayed, 'Oh God, please let me go!' It's amazing how God can get our attention. The very thing you said no to, you end up praying for! God said OK: 'Then the word of the LORD came to Jonah a second time: "Go to the great city of Nineveh and proclaim to it the message I give you" ' (Jonah 3:1–2). He was given a message he hadn't wanted to deliver: 'In forty days Nineveh will be overthrown.' God may give you a word you have to preach. It's not what you wanted to preach, but you do it because he tells you to. It hurts when things don't go according to our plans.

There is great potential in an unwanted calling. It refers to what you are capable of becoming. God sees what you are capable of being and saying. If you got to do only what you wanted to do, you wouldn't ever know your capability in another area. Your potential is what God sees, but you can't. God can see a potential in you which you can't see, so he leads you in a way which – at first – doesn't seem to make sense.

Take those who have felt their potential was being wasted because of the way they were led. How would you like to have been among those from the royal family in ancient Israel? What about those from the nobility, showing aptitude for learning, being well informed, quick to understand and qualified to serve in the King's palace? That was Daniel; that was also Shadrach, Meshach and Abednego (Dan. 1). They had to learn the language and the literature of the Babylonians. They

214

were held captive, taken to Babylon. Here were men who would have preferred to stay in Israel, but no. Because of their ability, they were captured and they had to learn things that they were not the slightest bit interested in: the language and literature of the Babylonians. But God made them legends.

Perhaps that is what has happened to you. You are forced to study things. You think, 'I didn't want to learn this! It's the last thing I was interested in!' God says, 'But you are going to need it one day!' 'I don't see how, this doesn't make sense!' you say.

Years later, Shadrach, Meshach and Abednego stood head and shoulders above others; they became legends – all because they wouldn't bow down to the golden image, and they were thrown into the burning fiery furnace. The King had said, 'Who is this God who will deliver you?' They said, as it were, 'We don't even have to think about that, O King. Our God is able to deliver us, but if he doesn't we won't bow down!' (see Dan. 3:16–18). It was their finest hour and they made history. We would never have heard of Shadrach, Meschach and Abednego if they had not been taken captive to Babylon. They stood out as a great testimony. Where was all their learning and expertise? Do you know what God had in mind for them? A strong faith. The potential to have a strong faith in God would not have been realised had they stayed in Jerusalem.

As for Daniel, because he was rising up the ranks, people were jealous of him. They threw him into the lions' den. It turns out that Daniel wasn't hurt by the lions and, at the King's command, the men who had falsely accused Daniel were brought in and thrown into the lions' den. The King wrote to all the peoples and all nations and men of every language and said, 'I issue a decree that in every part of my kingdom people must fear and reverence the God of Daniel. For he is the living God and he endures for ever; his kingdom will not be destroyed, his dominion will never end. He rescues and he saves; he performs signs and wonders in the heavens and on the earth. He has rescued Daniel from the power of the lions' (Dan. 6:26–7). There was a potential in Daniel that otherwise would never have been discovered.

'Moses was educated in all the wisdom of the Egyptians and was powerful in speech and action' (Acts 7:22). Then the next thing you know is that he has gone to visit his people, the children of Israel. You think, 'Well, what a waste.' He was educated in the wisdom of the Egyptians, but his career was going to be with his people, the Hebrews. Why did God do that? Moses would face the Pharaoh years later and he was trained in the wisdom of the Egyptians. He was brought up in the palace, he knew how the Pharaoh's mind worked. All that training that went back years before was now brought back at the moment when he was used.

The way we have been led we cannot understand at the time, but time shows there is purpose and meaning in it all. So with you. God knows your potential and it may seem wasted at first, but one day you will see a reason for all that you've learned and the explanation for all your training. What if you even sacrifice that career?

I think of T.W. Wilson. How many know who T.W.

Wilson is? Very few, probably. But do you know who Billy Graham is? T.W. is Billy's closest friend and personal aide. T.W. Wilson also happens to be a great preacher. He has preached for us at Westminster Chapel. We got George Beverley Shea to sing the same night that T.W. preached for us. T.W. Wilson has given a life to doing virtually nothing but carrying Billy Graham's suitcase. Wherever Billy goes, T.W. goes. Billy never stays in a hotel alone, T.W. is always there. This is partly how they have kept any malicious rumours from starting. T.W. is Billy Graham's shadow. But T.W. doesn't ever get asked to preach much these days; he sacrificed a career to be what Billy Graham needed. T.W. has no complaints. As for Billy himself, he had been president of a Christian college in Minneapolis, Minnesota, but he got so many invitations to preach that he left the college. Billy Graham's ministry was actually an unwanted calling. God also knows your potential. The potential of an unwanted calling is to show what you are capable of being and doing. The training by itself would never have revealed this.

What is the purpose of an unwanted calling? It is the reason for the thorn in the flesh in the first place. Paul said, 'To keep me from being conceited.' God directed you differently from what you wanted in order to give you the usefulness and intimacy with him you would not have otherwise experienced. If you are like me, you would have been too proud had you got what you wanted. I hate to think what my life would be like today if I hadn't remained at Westminster Chapel. It is not what I wanted. But that is not the whole story. Had I returned to America, I doubt I would have ever needed to know how to dignify a trial, to forgive those who've hurt me, to know how we can grieve the Holy Spirit by bitterness. These insights changed my life. I doubt I would have ever thought about things like that.

God's purpose is twofold. First, everything that he does in our lives is geared for one purpose, to know the Lord. 'I want to know Christ and the power of his resurrection and the fellowship of sharing in his sufferings, becoming like him in his death' (Phil. 3:10). I find it very interesting that Philippians was written after Paul had that disaster by going to Jerusalem (Acts 21–26). Nothing happened as he had hoped and he alludes to it in Philippians 1:12: 'Now I want you to know, brothers, that what has happened to me has really served to advance the gospel.' The Philippians were worried about him, but he says, 'As for what happened to me, it doesn't matter, it hasn't hurt the gospel.' It is as though he says, 'I may not be in good shape in some ways, but it advanced the gospel.' That's what it's all for. God doesn't care whether I am seen as a great success. He cares about one thing, that I get to know his Son. He says, 'R.T., I am sorry about having to disappoint you in some things, but there's only one way that you are going to get to know my Son and that is to put you through all this.'

Everything that has happened to us – whether it be an unwanted calling, living where we have to live, working with the people we have to work with, having to study one thing and having a career doing the opposite – is because God wants us to know his Son. The potential that you have for intimacy with God would never be discovered if you got to do what you wanted to do. If you had the success you wanted, you wouldn't be teachable. You can always tell a successful man, but you can't tell him much. God knows where to keep us. So when we get to the place where we say, 'I just want to know him,' God says, 'Good.'

But there is another purpose, and it is this: that we might have a reward at the judgment seat of Christ. It was so important to Paul:

> Do you not know that in a race all the runners
> run, but only one gets the prize? Run in such a
> way as to get the prize. Everyone who competes
> in the games goes into strict training. They do it
> to get a crown that will not last; but we do it to
> get a crown that will last for ever. Therefore I do
> not run like a man running aimlessly; I do not
> fight like a man beating the air. No, I beat my
> body and make it my slave so that after I have
> preached to others, I myself will not be
> disqualified for the prize (1 Cor. 9:24–7).

And, 'For I am already being poured out like a drink offering, and the time has come for my departure. I have fought the good fight, I have finished the race, I have kept the faith. Now there is in store for me the crown of righteousness, which the Lord, the righteous Judge, will award to me on that day – and not only to me, but also to all who have longed for his appearing' (2 Tim. 4:6–8).

In a word, the thorn of an unwanted calling is the best

thing that could have happened to any of us. We all need a thorn to save us from ourselves, and Paul could say at the end of the day, 'It's worth it all!' Or, as Joseph put it, 'God meant it for good.'

Conclusion

Three times I pleaded with the Lord to take it away from me. But he said to me, 'My grace is sufficient for you, for my power is made perfect in weakness.' (2 Cor. 12:8–9)

I am glad that Paul added these words. Except for this: he prayed only three times that his thorn would be removed; I myself have prayed hundreds of times about mine. I have sought the best counsel, been prayed for by the godliest people I could find. But when it finally dawned on me that my problem is best understood as a thorn in the flesh, I felt much, much better. Until then I blamed myself, thought there was something wrong with me, and that I wasn't spiritual enough (or otherwise it would have gone away).

And yet it is because I'm not spiritual enough that I have this thorn. Whether it will go away before I die, I don't know. But I now accept – and I really do believe this – that it is unquestionably the best thing that could have happened to me. I have become convinced that it has saved me from far more serious problems than I have already had. God knew exactly what it would take to keep me from being even more conceited than I am. '. . . for he knows how we are formed, he remembers that we are dust' (Ps. 103:14).

I could have made this book twice as long as it is. The list is endless as to various possibilities of what one's thorn in the flesh might be. For example, could not the feeling of guilt over past sin be a thorn? Even though we know God forgives, we have trouble forgiving ourselves. What about that person you have forgiven, but who will not forgive you – is this not a thorn in the flesh? What about children who have gone wrong and the parents blame themselves? What about a relationship that has gone sour, or that someone who has deserted you? What if you have been damaged by a spiritual authority figure? What about the person who is a product of a bad education? What if you had a bad parent? What about withheld success – or vindication withheld?

The big question I ask is: have you lived long enough to thank God for unanswered prayer? Presumably the reason Paul stopped praying about the removal of his problem after only three times is because the Lord stepped in and said: 'My grace is sufficient for you, for my power is made perfect in weakness' (2 Cor. 12:9). When Paul realised that that thorn in the flesh was God's instrument for a greater anointing, he was happy to stop praying further about it. After all, why abort the very thing that gives one more anointing?

A few years ago my wife and I were driving in Kentucky and on the radio came a country and western song called 'Thank God for Unanswered Prayer'. It was about a man who prayed and prayed years before that his childhood sweetheart would marry him. She wouldn't and never did. But years later he had not only found the wife of his dreams, but happened to see his old girlfriend some time after that. When he saw how she had turned out, he fell to his knees and thanked God for unanswered prayer!

I have lived long enough, as far as I can tell, to thank God for every unanswered prayer. That is, prayers prayed in the distant past. To be honest, I have offered prayers more recently that have gone on being unanswered (so far) which makes no sense to me at all. But I predict that, at the end of the day, I will have no complaints. God is not only sovereign, he is loving and gracious. No good thing does he withhold from those who sincerely try to do his will in everything (Ps. 84:11).

Unanswered prayer is still an enigma – that is, puzzling in the light of Jesus' words, 'You may ask me for anything in my name, and I will do it' (John 14:14). James said, 'You do not have, because you do not ask God', but added, 'When you ask, you do not receive, because you ask with wrong motives, that you may spend what you get on your pleasures' (Jas. 4:2–3). It follows from this that God does not answer prayers that are not in his will. After all, John said, 'This is the assurance we have in approaching God: that if we ask anything according to his will, he hears us. And if we know that he hears us – whatever we ask – we know that we have what we asked of him' (1 John 5:14–15).

I can only conclude that asking in Jesus' name must in some direct sense relate to God's will. There is a verse that haunts me, 'So he gave them what they asked for, but sent a wasting disease upon them' (Ps. 106:15). This may refer to the murmuring of the Children of Israel in the desert (Exod. 16) or it may refer to Israel's ill-posed request for a king (1 Sam. 8:6–7). I do know that God later said, 'So in my anger I gave you a king, and in my wrath I took him away' (Hos. 13:11).

The enigma of unanswered prayer lies in the apparent incongruity between what seems good to us at the time and what God knows is good for us. A few days before my mother died at the age of forty-three, my father thought God had revealed to him that she would be healed from the stroke that she had suffered a few weeks before. I too felt that God had shown me she would be healed. I was seventeen at the time, and when she died my father feared I would lose my faith. He kept saying, 'God is too wise to err, too kind to be unmerciful.'

Sometimes our prayers, which seem so right, flow from a faulty theology. When we are in love with our theological assumptions – and can't imagine they could be wrong – we tend to presume God surely agrees with us! The disciples asked the resurrected Christ, 'Lord, are you at this time going to restore the kingdom to Israel?' (Acts 1:6). It had not crossed their minds that Jesus never once planned to do anything of the kind.

Still worse is the assumption of some that, if we have enough faith, all our prayers will be answered. One famous 'health and wealth' preacher in America actually said publicly, 'If the apostle Paul had had my faith, he wouldn't have had his thorn in the flesh.' This kind of reasoning undermines the New Testament generally and

God's appointment of Paul particularly, who said, 'Whatever you have learned or received or heard from me, or seen in me – put it into practice. And the God of peace will be with you' (Phil. 4:9). God gave the early Church an apostle who was willing to let God be God – who has a will of his own and said, 'I will have mercy on whom I will have mercy' (Exod. 33:19). God is sovereign and has his own reasons as to why he gives or withholds mercy, and he does not have to explain himself to any of us.

Although unanswered prayer is a mystery, there is also an explanation. It is only a matter of time before we will be given an explanation. But it comes down to this: God has a better idea than that which we asked for. When Mary and Martha sent word to Jesus that his close friend (their brother) was sick, it did not cross their minds that Jesus would not come at once to heal Lazarus. He showed up four days after the funeral. Mary and Martha were heartbroken, if not bitter: 'if you had been here, my brother would not have died' (John 11:21). They wept openly and Jesus wept with them (John 11:35), even though he knew full well what he was about to do. He thought that raising Lazarus from the dead was a better idea than keeping him from dying (John 11:40, 43ff).

In the meantime, we all must accept God's verdict: painful though it is and puzzling though it is when we pray so hard for it to go away, the thorn in the flesh is in a sense our salvation; not that we are saved in the sense of going to heaven, but saved from ourselves.

When my mother was a little girl in her home town of Springfield, Illinois, she used to gather with other children in her church around a ninety-year-old lady who was loved by all. That lady once said this to them: 'I have served the Lord for so long now that I can hardly tell the difference between a blessing and a trial.' This is so true even if it means that the more the Lord uses us, the less we are able to enjoy it. But the increased anointing that flows as a result of the thorn is worth it all.

Notes

9 A chronic illness

1 See Judges 6:36–40, when Gideon asked for a sign from God by praying that the wool fleece be wet – then dry – as proof that God was truly with him.
2 Care for the Family, Garth House, Leon Avenue, Cardiff CF4 7RG.
3 In ancient Israel there was a belief that sickness was God's punishment because of sin in one's life, as was the assumption in the case of Job's accusers. This lay behind the situation in Job 9:2: 'Indeed, I know that this is true. But how can a mortal be righteous before God?'
4 Rodney Howard-Browne, a South African evangelist who now lives in America, has the ministry of 'laying on of hands' (Heb. 6:1–2). What became known as the 'Toronto Blessing' was traced to him.

11 Money matters

1 When Jesus said, 'Therefore I tell you, do not worry about your life, what you will eat or drink; or about your body, what you will wear. Is not life more important than food, and the

body more important than clothes?' (Matt. 6:25), he was not speaking against having money, but was assuring us that our heavenly Father will always supply our needs. He was telling us not to be overcome with worry when it comes to food, shelter and clothing. Our main concern is to be seeking God first, as we shall see below.

2 I would refer the reader to: Keith Tondeur, Credit action, 6 Regent Terrace, Cambridge CB2 1AA; tel. 01223 324 034. He has also written *Financial Tips for the Family* (Hodder & Stoughton); *What Price the Lottery?* (Monarch); *Your Money and Your Life* (Triangle); *What Jesus Said about Money and Possessions* (Monarch).

3 For further reading on this subject, see my *Gift of Giving* (Hodder & Stoughton, 1982).